Praise for

WHEN I MET FOOD

"*When I MET Food* is an honest and intimate walk through the life and brilliance of an exceptional businesswoman and lover of food with a heart of service. This type of first-hand account is rare and invaluable. Any budding chef, restaurateur, or business person of any field would be well served by reading this book, really *reading* this book. If you're paying attention, you will be handed a road map that few business people at Kathy Sidell's level share. But the sharing, after all, is the definition of hospitality."

—Tiffani Faison, chef/owner Sweet Cheeks,
Bravo's "Top Chef" season one finalist

"Kathy Sidell serves up a simple, straight-forward, and full-flavored homage to her love affair with food. Anyone considering a run at opening a restaurant or, for that matter, anyone who really enjoys restaurants will find *When I MET Food* an interesting and informative read."

—Roger Berkowitz, CEO and president of Legal Seafood

"*When I MET Food* takes you on a journey about the lifetime passion for food. Born into a family who not only dined out but helped to build the Boston restaurant scene, Kathy Sidell details how those early days shaped who she has become: a filmmaker, a wife, a mother, sister and daughter; and finally a successful restaurant owner several times over. For anyone dreaming of running their own restaurant, this book is must-read."

—Todd English, chef, restaurateur, author,
and James Beard Award winner

"If you've ever dreamed of opening your own restaurant, you'll love this book. And if you're a woman with restaurant ambitions, you absolutely need this book. Kathy Sidell distills a lifetime of hard-earned wisdom—her own and that of her legendary family—into this gracefully written narrative. Part memoir, part history of Boston's storied dining scene, it's also a must-read for any entrepreneur, both a pep talk and a wake-up call on what it takes to succeed."

—Amy Traverso, lifestyle editor of *Yankee Magazine* and author of *The Apple Lover's Cookbook*

"As a frequent diner at the MET's first restaurant (Kathy now has five), I am a huge fan of how Kathy has translated her vision onto the plate and into a thriving business. Her restaurant concepts are always on trend and offer quality and inspired dining experiences. ***When I MET Food*** beautifully captures her compelling journey."

—Tom Stemberg, Managing GP of Highland Consumer Fund and co-founder/former CEO of Staples

"Remarkable read...fresh and original, two characteristics I greatly appreciate. A success story to inspire all but more importantly for me it is told with great skill and without apology."

—Robert Richardson award-winning cinematographer

"Kathy Sidell has created a memoir of a life filled with passion and love for family, friends, art, and food. Her story is woven with the common thread of food. This book is peppered with fun recipes and stories that include many people I know, especially her father, Jack, a man I greatly admired, and, who enabled me to start my first restaurant, but there is much more to this book. Restaurateurs and want-to-be's should pay special attention to some amazing pearls of wisdom in these pages; there are very keen insights into the balance of art and commerce, as well as practical advice resulting from a philosophy that has brought Kathy great success."

—Jasper White, chef/ partner Summer Shack Restaurants

WHEN I MET FOOD

WHEN I MET FOOD

LIVING THE AMERICAN RESTAURANT DREAM

KATHY SIDELL

bibliomotion
books + media

First published by Bibliomotion, Inc.
33 Manchester Road
Brookline, MA 02446
Tel: 617-934-2427
www.bibliomotion.com

Printed in the United States of America

Library of Congress Cataloging-in-Publication Data

Sidell, Kathy.
    When I met food : living the American restaurant dream / Kathy Sidell.
        pages cm
    ISBN 978-1-937134-31-0 (hardcover : alk. paper)—ISBN
978-1-937134-32-7 (ebook)—ISBN 978-1-937134-33-4 (enhanced ebook)
    1. Sidell, Kathy.   2. Restaurateurs—Massachusetts—Biography.
I. Title.
    TX910.5.S58A3 2012
    647.95092—dc23
    [B]
                                2012033788

For Carl, my true life partner,
For Alexandra and Benjamin, my most treasured accomplishments,
For Mom, the woman who had a remarkable vision for my life,
And to my Dad, for his undeniable DNA.

Acknowledgments

Writing this book has been an intriguing journey. I discovered things along the way that surprised me, or that I hadn't had the chance to articulate out loud yet. It has been a unique opportunity to take stock, and think deeply about my life and my business—about where I have been and where I am going. I hope that the end result resonates for anyone interested in the hospitality business and that they will find it a worthy read.

For those of you that helped bring *When I MET Food* to fruition:

I want to thank Charlotte and Deb for the introduction to Erika and Jill. Erika and Jill, for believing that I had a story to tell. Without their continual prodding there would be no book and I would surely still be questioning if I had a viable story to tell. A special thank you to Stephanie Land for her abject talent, patience, and ability to take my story and help me make it sing, which would not have been possible without her. And to Deb VA for your friendship and for always protecting me, ferociously.

For those of you in my life daily:

I want to deeply thank my loving, patient husband Carl for making my restaurant dreams come true and sacrificing things he might have dreamed of for himself, like early retirement. And for finally understanding the way in which I move—and embracing it. Life together has been an amazing unexpected journey.

To my children, Benjamin and Alexandra, the sheer loves of my life and about whom I am deeply proud and with whom life is at its most powerful and most connected. I learn from you both every day, which is an amazing gift. There are very few people's company I enjoy more. You remain my most treasured accomplishments.

Deep gratitude for my Mom for the way we *get* each other. She has had a remarkable vision for my life and the lives of my children for which I feel deeply blessed and eternally grateful. She has made me a stronger, better human being with her sage guidance and has been my most stolid supporter.

To Dad, who is watching from above—and who may finally see me! Our relationship taught me that wanting someone's approval can translate to deep ambition. You are with me every day, Papa Jack. I think you have turned into my guardian angel. You taught me more than you, sadly, will ever know.

My true inspiration, Stephanie, an extraordinary role model, a chosen and much cherished older sister, with whom life has much more meaning and through whom I have learned to recognize that people have differences and to love them in spite of those.

And to all the girls in my life who have shown me the way and who continue to inspire, nurture, and encourage: Nana, Kitty, Mom, Alexandra, Stephanie, Courtney, Lindsey, Madeleine, Wendy, Karen, Auntie, Stacey, Renee, Trustman, Molly, Ellie G, Lulu, Cindy, Jayne, Heidi, Leslie, Marion, Lisa and Jane, Deb VA, Natalie, Emily, Eva, Cynthia, Scout, Stephanie M,

ACKNOWLEDGMENTS

Suzanne, Ellen K, Tiffani, and Marianne. And the extraordinary girls many of you have created. Some are mentioned in the book, some not, all equally important.

And to all the men who have made my journey vastly more interesting. That might be the next book.

For those in my work life:

To Jamie, Todd, Mark, Stephen, and Jennifer, without whom I would never have been able to get to this point. I have cherished every moment—the good, the bad, and the ugly—but most of all, our fabulous food adventures.

To all the people who lives that touch mine along the way—to the chefs, managers, bar tenders, food runners, hosts, back waiters, dishwashers, valet parkers. The many staff who help run the well-oiled machines at the MET restaurants, hour after hour, day after day, month after month. It has been a privilege to meet and be part of your lives, and I hope you have learned as much from me as I have from you.

And last but not least to the many of the guests that have taken refuge in any one of our restaurants. I am eternally grateful to have had the chance to serve and feed you. I hope we met (even surpassed) your expectations and that if we didn't that you told me about it. And to many of the patrons that have become good friends and who have allowed us to build a community, you have been incredibly supportive and an essential part of what we have been working so hard to build.

Thank you all so very much.

Gratefully, Kathy.

Contents

Introduction

For the past few months I've been trying to invent a new word. "Foodie" is a perfectly adequate way to describe people who love food. But there are people who love food, and then there are those of us who are ruled by it. We can be an irrational, unreasonable, obsessive lot when it comes to making that crucial decision of what to eat for a snack, let alone dinner. My mother is fond of saying that I would travel many miles to find a fresh fig or date. She exaggerates, but not by much. The feelings that wash over me when I bite into a perfectly grilled piece of summer corn or the anticipation I experience when spearing a forkful of oozing burrata paired with a sliver of salty prosciutto—it's no hyperbole to compare it to a spiritual experience.

The word "foodie" just doesn't seem expressive enough to describe people like me. There are other more classic options, of course, but none of them fit the bill either. A gourmet, gastronome, or epicure sounds annoyingly effete and preoccupied by her own good taste and refinement. I know enough to savor a bottle of Chateau d'Yquem, but I will just as happily drink an inexpensive bottle of lambrusco on a hot summer night; I love white truffles laced through fine pasta but will also gnaw on a barbecued pork rib until I've ingested every last scrap of meat and fat and pure goodness.

So what's the word? Food–ista, as I call myself on my Twitter handle? Too flip. Foodslut? Too dirty. What about combining the Latin roots for food and passion: Cibusamor? Too... Latin. The new word should imply hedonism and evoke drama. It should be visceral and sensual, even onomatopoetic, like the happy huffing sounds we make when we've stuffed ourselves so much we can't breathe. Whatever that word is, that's what I am. And for the past eight years, I've made it my business to translate that experience to as many people as possible.

Born into a family where every meal was an event and where food was the conduit for love, I learned at an early age that there is power in the simple act of feeding people. Yet, though I am a passionate cook, my dream was never to be chef at my restaurants. I spend a lot of time in our kitchens, watching (some would say like a hawk), teaching, tasting, and above all maintaining quality and consistency—two hallmarks of any exceptional restaurant—but I would never want to spend my entire career there. First of all, being a chef is grueling work that demands hours on your feet. I got into the business when I was forty-seven. I'm in good shape, but not that good. There is no harder job in the world, and I am in awe of the speed and skill with which our chefs and line cooks execute my vision every day.

Second, and more importantly, my skills are better suited on the other side of the line. A big part of any successful career is knowing your strengths. When conducting interviews, I often ask applicants to tell me where they feel most comfortable—expediting in the kitchen, managing the bar, seating the dining room from the host stand, or tending to guests. I for one am a people person. I'd be miserable hidden away in the back of the house because much of the pleasure I get out of cooking hinges on watching people enjoy what I've prepared. I am an observer, maybe even a voyeur. As a restaurateur, I get to indulge my culinary imagination by planning menus, and I get to closely interact with my guests. I'm more macro than micro, preferring to spend my time considering the big picture, working hard to understand my guests' wants and desires, cooking up concepts that have mass appeal, and figuring out how to turn them into something concrete and profitable.

I was a double major in English literature and theater, and I attended graduate school at Columbia University to study film. I am drawn to good storytelling and I process the world in vignettes and images; I love to analyze data but I would never want to have to collect it. In other words, I am not your typical businesswoman. What I am is a student of the world. I have watched and learned as people close to me opened and closed restaurants and food-related businesses, and I stowed the lessons I gleaned from their experience into my mental filing cabinet until I was ready to strike out on my own. My goal was never to open just one great restaurant—that's an exceedingly hard way to make money. My goal was to grow a great restaurant business that would give me the freedom to incorporate all of the lessons I've learned over the years about food, human nature, hospitality, and entrepreneurship. I wanted to deliver a high-quality dining experience, and I wanted to make money while doing it. Some people might look down on that, but there is an art to feeding people at the scale and quality that I do. And there is never any shame in making money doing something you love. It's especially nice when you can do it in a place that you love, as well.

I have traveled the world over, and while there are places that feel like home to me like Nantucket, Los Angeles, and Rome, I am a Bostonian through and through. You can take the girl out of Boston, but you can't take the Boston out of the girl. I was born and raised here, and in spite of my father's best efforts to eradicate my accent, on occasion you can hear it when I replace the "er" at the end a word with an "a." I love this city for all its strengths and frailties, and I can't imagine living anywhere else. It's not easy to get a feel for Bostonians—we're discreet. Maira Kalman, the artist famous for capturing the vibrancy of life in her amazing illustrations of New York City, might have a hard time drawing Boston. To look at us, there's nothing that makes us particularly distinct. In New York, dressing and behaving in a way to get noticed is a prerequisite to living there. I recently returned from Austin and the cowboy hipster vibe there is unmistakable. But Boston is ball caps and t-shirts. We are a preppy city, a conservative city, and an intellectual city. We're sports maniacs. We don't ever go too far this way or that, except when we're frothing at the mouth during a Red Sox game at Fenway Park or tailgaiting in twenty-degree weather at Gillette stadium. My identification with this city, and my deep affection for it and its residents, has been a key reason why locals have embraced my restaurants, even as the business gains an international reputation. Do what you love, but whenever possible, do it where you love to spend the majority of your time, too. It makes life so sweet.

When I look at the four restaurants that I've launched, and the fifth that will be newly opened by the time this book is published, I'm proud of what I see. They are well-reviewed, and they are always full. They are the culmination of the hunger, both literal and figurative, that has always been my driving force. Though I had worked in the film industry for more than twenty years by the time I opened my first restaurant in Chestnut Hill, a suburb about six miles outside of Boston, getting into the business felt as natural as getting up in the morning. Everything was so new, but at the risk of sounding like Shirley MacLaine, I was certain I had done this job before. That is how damned comfortable it felt despite how daunting the experience was. Though I had gleaned a great deal from my father and sister, both already deeply entrenched in the restaurant world, there was a lot I still didn't know. And yet, I seemed to understand the essence of the business at my core. It's something I was born to do.

After only eight years as a restaurateur, I'm a relative newcomer to the scene and I still have a lot left to learn. The world doesn't often reward us for slowing down, yet I see value in pausing mid flight to take stock and contemplate where I have been and where I am going. It also gives me the chance to pay homage to the people who have helped me get so far so fast. That's why I've included so many recipes in this book. Some are from my own restaurants, but the majority are dishes that I associate with the people who have inspired me and helped mold me into who I am. I'm that person who stays behind in the movie theater to watch the very last name scroll up the screen—it's important to acknowledge people and to give credit where it's due. So thanks, Mom. And Carl. And Dad. And Stephi. If I've learned anything, it's that success isn't just a result of strategy and good business sense, but of being willing to learn from others and drawing from the lessons life has to teach us as we muddle our way through.

In addition, perhaps I can offer some guidance and inspiration to others who might be considering a similar career. Though life is unpredictable and random, and the creative process is specific to each individual, there are universal rules to building a successful restaurant or business: Be who you are. Don't worry about what the competition is doing. Believe in your concept and stick to it. Learn the art of the deal, and learn to say no. Watch your downside. Buy your own real estate if you can. Understand your brand and bring everything back to it. And always settle in the corner. Take those truths to heart and you can translate them into a successful restaurant business. I'm living proof.

What didn't work out the way I thought it would? What have been the pleasant surprises? Now that I've seen how life can take one's best laid plans and throw them around like an energetically tossed salad, what considerations will I make going forward from here? That's what I hope to find out. And I hope the answers I uncover will help illuminate the path for anyone else thinking of acting on their own restaurant dreams.

One

Serving Up Happiness

In my life, food has always been a family affair, and the fact that I have opened five well-received restaurants doesn't keep my mother from giving me a piece of her mind when she spots something that doesn't conform to her exacting standards of what is worth eating and what is not. Lately we've had a running battle over Marshmallow Fluff. At my second restaurant, MET Bar & Grill, we sometimes serve a peanut butter cake with Fluff on top, and occasionally Fluff makes a crowning appearance on our ice cream sundaes. My mother, whose elegant dinner parties are legendary, sees it on the menu and becomes apoplectic. "Disgusting!" she once said, wrinkling her perfect nose. "How can you serve it? No one eats that." Calmly, or as calmly as anyone can be in the face of criticism from one's mother, I pointed out to her that when Fluff shows up on the menu, it is our top-selling dessert, so someone does, in fact, want to eat it.

My father was even worse. When I opened my first restaurant, the Metropolitan Club, he was convinced that we should top our French fries with a creamy layer of raclette, a type of cheese ubiquitous in Switzerland, traditionally melted over potatoes. I did not remind him that he had already tried that at

1

his restaurant, Pomme Frite, which had failed. Instead, I tried to be tactful and merely pointed out that few Americans knew what raclette was and that it was unlikely to sell well. He still took offense, like it was an insult to the entire Swiss populace that the rest of the world didn't appreciate their national dish. And then there was the borscht. How could I think that, when considering their Friday night dinner options, most of Boston wasn't craving a bowl of borscht with sour cream?

My father was a brilliant businessman with a phenomenal gift for spotting culinary talent, but if he had a flaw it was that he took food so personally—he couldn't accept that there was a bigger America out there that didn't want to eat the foods that made his heart sing, or that disagreed with his idea of how food should be prepared. Though he was instrumental in launching today's Boston restaurant scene by financing many rising star chefs, his refusal to reconcile his tastes with those of the general public would ultimately hamstring his own restaurant dreams. Part of what makes me good at what I do comes from having watched him try and fail to bend the American palate to his will.

For my parents, Jack and Barbara Sidell, there was a right way to eat and a wrong way, and their way was always right. Many years before he would back the likes of Todd English and Jasper White, my father tried to open several establishments of his own. One was called J. Victor's (his full name was James Victor Sidell), which he opened in a space previously held by Purcell's, an old-school saloon popular with Boston's bankers and lawyers. It evoked a fantasy version of a 1930s steak house, heavy on thick cuts of meat and old favorites like three-bean salad. Dad also included his deservedly famous brisket on the menu. Rumor has it that someone once called my father to the table to complain that the brisket was a little tough. To this, my father replied, "I hope you choke on it." J. Victor's closed in a little less than eighteen months.

It is a great irony that someone so skilled in spotting talent, someone who could put chefs on the map, wasn't cut out to be a restaurateur. But not many people are, though you wouldn't know it to look at the explosion of newly opened restaurants all around the country. The world is a different place than it was when Dad first tried to open his restaurants in the late seventies. Those of us operating today have the advantage of an audience that knows food in a bigger and better way, one that has traveled more and been exposed to food 24–7 thanks to the Food Network. Cooking has become an eagerly followed spectator sport, and the proliferation of restaurants in every city parallels this awareness and growing interest, and probably reinforces it. Despite the recession, Boston alone created more than eleven thousand restaurant seats in 2011—more than there have ever been. That number represents a lot of people attempting to turn their restaurant dreams into reality.

Why do so many people want to open their own restaurant? Whether they are chefs looking for a showcase for their talents, entrepreneurs, or both, there is something undeniably romantic and exciting about the restaurant world. It's not just about wanting to feed people your favorite foods. It's about establishing a legacy. Travelers walking into a bar or restaurant in an unfamiliar city for the first time experience a living snapshot of that city's time and place. As a restaurateur, you contribute to the movement and evolution of your city, and if you can create something that's signature, you and your restaurant have the potential to become not only part of its fabric, but part of its history.

Food has become a major part of American social currency. You can learn a lot about people from what they eat, and what a person orders in a restaurant is often a reflection of his taste, lifestyle, and status. Food is a path to finding kindred spirits. Where have you been? Did you try that dish? Did you love it? Where, how, and what we eat has become a way for people to define themselves, which means that today the purveyors of that experience, the successful restaurateur or the heralded chef at a well-loved restaurant, holds a certain level of power and influence over the culture. That can be an intoxicating proposition.

But most people underestimate just how difficult owning a restaurant really is, and many of those newly opened restaurants of 2011 will falter and close. Though the success rate for new restaurants is not quite the commonly cited and dramatically abysmal one out of ten, the number of restaurants that make it past their first year still hovers near 40 percent. Why? Is it the food? Bad food will kill your place for sure, but food is not always the primary reason people frequent a restaurant. Besides, we can all think of wonderful restaurants serving great food that opened and closed within two or three years. So the formula for success must be a little more complicated than, "If you cook it, they will come." Critical success is worthless if it doesn't lead to financial success. The problem is that too many people fall victim to their own press and lose sight of the fact that they're not just running a restaurant, they are running a business.

What really makes or breaks a restaurant is not the food or the talent in the kitchen. It lies in everything the restaurant owner brings to the table, such as good business sense and good management technique, as well as in the multitude of business decisions she must make every day. These include immediate concerns such as the menu, service, atmosphere, or location, and long-range planning like marketing, branding, design, or growth strategy. That is, every decision affecting the restaurant. The people who make it in this business—both pure business entrepreneurs and chef-owners—are a special breed who balance a hard-to-come-by combination of finely honed business, social, psychological, and sensory skills.

There is room for variation, of course. One of my strengths

is multitasking, for example. My ability to juggle many things at once, including a dual career in film and food, has been intrinsic to any success I've achieved. Stretching yourself just shy of too thin doesn't work for everyone, though. My sister believes in doing one thing at a time, and doing it perfectly. That's a strategy that has worked brilliantly for her—she runs two of the most revered restaurants in Boston, Stephanie's on Newbury and Stephi's on Tremont. Which just goes to show that there is never just one way to achieve success. Overall, however, there are a few characteristics that most people who thrive in the business do share.

In many ways, my father fit the profile. Running a successful restaurant requires passion, vision, and business acumen, all of which he possessed in abundance. You also have to have strong people skills. Telling patrons they can choke on their brisket is a good way to make sure your doors close prematurely, but my father's cantankerousness was usually tempered by his vast amounts of charm.

Papa Jack's Brisket

Serves 8-10

1 double 5-6 pound beef brisket
3 tablespoons flour
Salt and pepper to taste
Canola oil for sautéing
1 quart veal stock
4 bottles of a flavorful beer (I use Heineken)
1 large Spanish onion, sliced
6 carrots, peeled and cut on the diagonal
3 tablespoons ketchup

1. Preheat the oven to 350 degrees.
2. Cover brisket with flour, salt, and pepper.
3. Put oil in a large sauté pan and heat. Once the pan is hot, place the brisket in the pan and sear on all sides until golden brown.
4. Place brisket in a large roasting pan. To the roasting pan add the veal stock and the beer, the sliced onions, and the carrots. Spread ketchup over top of brisket.
5. Cover and place pan in the oven. Cook for 3 hours. After 3 hours, remove the cover from the pan and cook for another half hour.
6. Remove the brisket from the pan and let it rest on a carving board for 30 minutes. Take the remaining stock, reduce and season, and use it as gravy for the brisket. Make sure to carve the brisket against the grain.

———————

It is also, of course, crucial to have an impeccable palate (his was excellent; my mother's is unsurpassed). In fact, all of your senses should be hyper-acute. If the bartender is smashing bottles your guests will feel like they're sitting near the Dumpster; if your waiter passes by with a platter of fried calamari your nose should be able to tell you instantly whether the oil it was fried in is as fresh as it should be; and you should be willing to test twenty different place settings to ensure that the fork, knife, and spoon design you choose feels perfectly weighted and balanced in your guests' hands. Your eyes must see beyond what the normal person sees, whether it's a crumb speck on the carpet that needs to be removed or a couple lingering over empty dessert plates, whose locked eyes and intertwined fingers signal that a warming digestif might be much appreciated. That's why, though the corner offers the best view, it's important that an owner sit in as many different spots as possible to see the walls, the carpet, the windows, and everything else in the restaurant from multiple angles. And you really do have to sit. It's not enough to keep your eyes open while you're moving through the restaurant at flash speed. Only by sitting quietly and patiently can you spot the tiny things that no one else will see—the light dust piling up a little on the mantle; small chips in the paint; a chair that seems to be tilting slightly. Sitting enables you to put a magnifying glass on the maintenance and service of that part of the room. In addition, if I don't sit in every banquette and every chair, I won't know when they need to be re-covered. If I haven't sat in a certain waitperson's section for a while, I won't know that her attention to detail isn't what it once was, and that she has started letting too much time go by before resilvering (putting out fresh silverware as needed) or leaving her water pitcher out in plain sight.

And then there is the financial reality. Though he considered himself an entrepreneur above everything else, my father was first a commercial lender, then a banker. The restaurant business is not for someone with a mere dollar and a dream. You need lots of dollars, and if you don't have them yourself you must find someone who will give or loan them to you. As far as I can tell there is only one thing that is guaranteed in the restaurant world, and that is that everything will cost more than you thought possible. Many wonderful restaurants have closed because the owners thought the quality of the food was all that really mattered. But gorgeous food is what initially gets a restaurant noticed and helps it build a loyal band of patrons. Money is what enables a restaurant owner to make the business secure, and to put into place the building blocks that will allow the restaurant to evolve and survive for years to come. Too many people fail to accept that their pockets may not be deep enough to support their endeavor. Although there are few rules that can be universally applied to any restaurant, there are at least two that hold up every time. This is one of them:

You must be able to cover your downside if the business takes a while to catch on, so you always have to raise more money—a lot more—than you think you're going to need. What kind of capital that represents varies, of course, but the formula is pretty simple: Consider your square footage. Calculate how many seats you can fit into that square footage, how many times you think you can turn each table, and what you believe your average ticket price will be. Seats x 4 x $35 = Daily Gross. This should help inform you as to what your potential gross per year might be. That number guides all your other costs—what you can afford for rent, labor, insurance, utilities, operational supplies, smallwares, repairs and maintenance, marketing, and training. Ultimately, the key is to cover your downside, be conservative, and count on making a lot less money than you want to at first. Unfortunately, not many people want to accept that reality.

Those that can, and who are willing to practice good fiscal discipline and err on the conservative side, should be in a good position to face all of their anticipated costs. The real challenge lies in having enough liquidity around to cover the *un*anticipated costs, and trust me, no matter how prepared you are, they happen. You move in and discover that your HVAC system is no longer working, or that your walk-in needs a new compressor, or you realize that you forgot to factor in your bar smallwares when calculating your bar budget. What kind of capital you'll need depends on the size and scale of the place you're opening, but it would probably be safe to have an additional 15 to 20 percent of your operating expenses available in working capital. Even the most prudent of us are usually too optimistic when we calculate our budgets. We want to believe that we're only going to spend $15,000 on beer, wine, and liquor and then we're shocked when it turns out we're spending $30,000. I'm opening a restaurant in Nantucket and the shipping charges are turning out to be far higher than I anticipated. There are costs that hide between the cracks of your budget, and there's no way you can address them until they sprout and make themselves noticed. No matter how much experience you have, each location brings with it expenses you haven't anticipated.

Stamina is important, too. There may be no crying in fine dining, but there's no sleep, either. A restaurateur should be in her restaurant physically, mentally, and emotionally every day, every night. She is obsessed and possessed, and, come to think of it, a bit of a masochist, too. Why else would you spend more than ten minutes in an environment where you are judged every day and every dish, and so ferociously? Food is primal. Food is survival. People take very little more seriously and more personally than their food. Even those with no interest in cooking have a great interest in dissecting and defending their version of their favorite dishes. And in this day, where criticism has transcended the domain of food journalists to anyone with a smart phone or a blog, it takes a tough disposition and a thick skin to keep on in the face of the cacophony of differing opinions.

And last, there is the other cardinal rule of the restaurant world, one that my father, for all his genius in the business world, failed to appreciate. If you want to run a restaurant—a successful one, where guests come back again and again—you have to embrace unconditionally and wholeheartedly what should be every restaurateur's mission: though you will never be able to please everyone, you will die trying. This Sisyphean challenge provides me with a near daily dose of my greatest pleasure, and occasionally my greatest pain.

From my father's successes and failures, I learned that my job is to not only put things on the menu that I love, but to recognize what other people love, too, and accommodate them. From my guests, I've learned that:

Everyone wants something for free.
Everyone wants to feel like a celebrity.

Everyone wants to be well taken care of.
Everyone wants to own a restaurant.
Everyone's mother can do it better.

I do my best to remember these realities every day that I come to work.

A restaurant's success may be partially about the food, the décor, and the price, but it is always all about the guest. You can serve the most brilliant food in the world and nobody will care if you forget that fact. Restaurateurs are not in the food industry, they are in the service industry. We are merely professional hosts, and without the guests, those who perpetuate the business, there is no party.

So, a fantastic palate, business savvy, deep pockets, thick skin, patience with criticism, and a desire to please that stems from the core, plus a natural talent for marketing and branding: this is the unique blend of attributes that make a person particularly suited for the restaurant business. They also happen to be characteristics that I possess. How did I come to acquire them? It's as though every step I've taken was specifically designed to give me the experiences I'd need to help me succeed in the life I lead now.

I met food a long time ago, and since then my whole life has revolved around it. No matter where I've been or what I've been doing, my mind has not strayed far from the thought of what my next meal would be. Some people talk about getting so busy they forget to eat. I can't say I know what that's like, and I've been a film producer—you don't get much busier. Even at the height of my film career, my copies of *Variety* and *The Hollywood Reporter* were intermixed with copies of *Gourmet*, *Saveur*, and *Food & Wine*. Whether I was dishing out homemade granola from my college dorm room, loading platters of chunky chicken salad in my sister's food shop, producing movies and documentaries, or shooting commercials on location in Belize,

I have always found a way to eat well and make sure the people around me eat well, too. If there is no restaurant nearby, I'll find a kitchen and get busy. Feeding people is how I communicate, how I bond with people. It was only natural that when I decided I was ready to launch my own business it would be in one that revolves around food. They say that you should do what you love, and there's nothing I love more than being with people I enjoy and sharing food with them.

At my five Boston area restaurants—The Metropolitan Club, two MET Bar & Grills, MET Back Bay, and MET on Main in Nantucket—the menus are long and the portions are hearty. I am and have always been The Everything Girl. I love abundance, I love choice and generosity, and that's what I want to provide my guests. I suppose if my dad's flaw was taking his food too personally, mine is probably that I have a hard time restraining myself. I knew when I opened my restaurants that I wanted to serve the best of what I had eaten in my life. I have been fortunate to be surrounded by a lot of great chefs and to frequent extraordinary restaurants since I was very young, and I wanted to duplicate that experience for others.

A lifetime of frequent traveling has given me the opportunity to experience an unseemly amount of delicious cuisine and to dine in some of the best restaurants in the world. Our best-selling duo of tuna and salmon tartare was inspired by an afternoon of sitting on the terrace at a deliciously fun restaurant in Paris on Avenue Montaigne called L'Avenue, owned by the same people who own Hotel du Cap. There's nowhere better to have a cold bottle of Brillicart Salmon champagne and a late afternoon snack while watching the world go by. As I ate their duo of tuna and salmon tartare, I realized that with a little "Met"amorphosis it would be a perfect everyday dish to introduce to Boston. With its low calories, light bite, and satisfyingly bold flavors, it quickly became our single top-selling dish among women (when my pants begin to feel a little tight,

I eat it every day). In fact, the tartare was so successful that I incorporated a tartare bar in our concept in Nantucket.

We also serve a knockout bone-in veal Parmesan in a gorgeous tomato sauce, so big it covers the plate. That dish was inspired by a version that made me swoon at the El San Juan in Puerto Rico, where the proprietor, upon hearing that I was about to open my first restaurant, sagely warned me, "Beware, people want everything for free." He turned out to be right, but at the time all I cared about was figuring out how I could bring this dish to Boston so that everyone I knew could try it. It had what I call the "Wow" factor, which is a level of surprise and delight that I seek to incorporate at every level of my restaurants, from the design to the flavor to the presentation to the service.

My culinary director Todd Winer and I keep lists of a variety of items we want to see on our menus, and we'll get together, narrow the list down, and start to develop recipes to make them our own. But even as we do, we constantly ask ourselves an important question, one that every restaurant must ask again and again: Who are we? Though the ingredients are exotic, have we made this dish American enough? Diners do not come to me to experiment. They come because they enjoy experiencing classic dishes served with a refined, modern touch, not because I can cook sous-vide foie gras. But I can, so though they may not arrive prepared to eat foie gras, when they see that they can try Hudson Valley foie gras on a burger, they do. In fact, they eat a lot of them—that particular burger sells well.

When deciding whether to include whisky-buttered cipollinis on a menu, I have to ask, do Americans know what cipollinis are? Should I call them baby onions instead? Menu wording is an art form in and of itself. To keep something fabulous off the menu would feel like I was short-changing my guests, but so would offering anything that didn't fit perfectly within the expectations I have set with the MET brand. We Americanize our dishes in a way that's relatable. At my restaurants you'll find the core of the American dining experience: we consistently deliver simple food made with great ingredients, and there are times we do it for twelve hundred people a day.

You'll find cipollinis at other steak houses or local suburban restaurants now, but you wouldn't have eight years ago. We were on the cutting edge of these concepts. I discovered that Americans are interested in eating all kinds of delicious things if you introduce it to them in language they understand. It's not just about taste making, introducing gorgeous new flavor and texture combinations, and innovative cooking techniques. Being a restaurant owner is also about taste spotting, always scanning the horizon to see what people are gravitating toward. I've been doing that since I was a child. When I meet people, one of the first things I want to know is what they've eaten recently.

When I travel, I've been known to hit four or five restaurants in one night. Were I just interested in cooking and food, my investigations would have been only fodder for my own creativity in the kitchen. But these obsessive pursuits, unbeknownst to me, have actually been research into why people eat the way they do and what they are interested in trying next, and this understanding eventually manifested itself on my menus. There's what I love, and then there's what people are going to love if they get the chance to try it, and finding the opportunities to offer it to them in an unforgettable, can't-wait-to-have-it-again way. What are people ready to try, they just don't know it yet? Thirty years ago, only the adventurous were patronizing Greek and Korean restaurants. But by the time I was ready to open the MET Bar & Grill, I could see that ordinary Bostonians had embraced Korean and Greek flavors. Kimchi or tzatziki . . . on a burger! Why not?

When I dreamed about the restaurant I would someday

open, I envisioned a place that would remind us why the classics are classic, bringing the past into the present while adding surprising twists. My food would be cooking, not cuisine, playful and modern, but not intimidating. There would be room for experimentation, but nothing truly out there like foam or liquid nitrogen (although we have been known to use meat glue). Because while I wanted to dance around the edges and introduce my guests to food they'd never had before or ingredients new to the American landscape, I also wanted to offer them something that they understood, and evoke a sense of comfort and belonging. For those already familiar with the items I'd offer, I hoped my food would in some way reawaken the same kind of good memories that inspired me to include them on the menu. And for those to whom everything was new, I would do my best to become the good memory itself.

The desire to continue to provide great memories for my guests is what keeps me obsessively reading, eating, researching, and seeking out new dining experiences. And watching. I'm in constant observation mode, looking, seeing, and learning. When I'm in town, you'll find me visiting my establishments every day, every night, seven days a week, making sure we maintain our standards while also seeking out opportunities to improve. No matter how much you're doing right, you can always do better. The pressure to perform perfectly every time in an industry where the variables change every day can be exhausting, but I love what I do anyway. Restaurants are where I belong. There's always something new going on, and I want to have a front-row seat. Truth be told, I'm not only keeping an eye on operations, I'm there for the show.

My son, who is an actor, and I have often joked about producing *Restaurant: The Musical!*, a kind of *Sunday in the Park with George* for restaurant-goers instead of art lovers. It would open on an empty stage, and the audience would watch a restaurateur slowly transform the space from an old empty shell to a vibrant, lively place brimming with texture and color and life. Through the score and lyrics she would reveal the workings of her imagination and a concept would unfold, followed by the design, the architecture, and the lighting. The personnel who breathe life into the space and infuse it with its singular vibe would take the stage. Then, in would come the guests, because a restaurant is nothing without its patrons, and the real drama would ensue. Only at the end would the food make a grand entrance.

I love movies and storytelling, and every night that you open the doors of your restaurant is like opening night, waiting for the screen to light up. I get the same sense of anticipation and excitement as I look around at the staff, poised on their marks, ready to spring into action. The tables are set. The lights are aglow. What's tonight going to bring?

Everything. Everything happens in restaurants—the BFF lunches, the father-daughter reunions, the first dates, last dates, engagements, and breakups. The reconciliation coffees, the neutral territory custody discussions, the internet hookups, the after-work drinks, the pre-theater apps, the business meetings, and the celebratory dinners. A good restaurateur spends every waking minute doing her best to make sure her restaurant is exactly what people need it to be at any given time. The task is at once debilitating and exhilarating. And when you see these people choose your restaurant as the setting for more than one of these moments, it is an honor.

One of the things I love about movies and theater is how you can watch ten seemingly independent stories, only to discover in the end that they are all interconnected in some way. From the front of the house of my restaurants I am privy to an endless series of vignettes taking place at this two-top or that booth, in the kitchen, at the bar, or in the bathroom. (In fact, when I first opened I used to sit in the bathroom stall, listening to the conversations around me. Women talk a lot, and in this way I learned a tremendous amount about my customers and my restaurants.) The guests are such a fascinating part of the business, particularly when you're in a neighborhood environment and you know 90 percent of the people coming through the door. They become the characters of your nightly reality show. The neighborhood dentist who is a self-proclaimed oenophile; the owner of a local sports team and his coach, who religiously eat the same dish night after night; the couple that never does anything but fight—where shall we seat them tonight? I love being in the center of the action, witness to life taking place, to people connecting, fighting, loving, and laughing.

As I write, the show has already begun at my restaurant in the beautiful Back Bay neighborhood in Boston. It is loud here in the cozy Library Bar, the din almost deafening. In honor of the unseasonably mild winter weather we have opened the patio, which can feel a bit like opening a whole new restaurant for all the tables it adds. Perhaps we should have waited, for it's Friday night of Restaurant Week and we already had two hundred people on the books. Now we also have a crush of walk-ins who saw the patio open and are anxious to have their first al fresco meal of the year. We are in the midst of a perfect storm and we are not prepared. I hear a waiter mention that the kitchen has run out of Restaurant Week desserts. It is only 8 P.M. I hear the crash of glasses in the nearby wait station, and silver getting tossed about. How many will disappear into the trash? I see that my general manager, who is supposed to be touching tables to check in with guests, is frantically bussing tables. I see nothing but potential disaster—we have run out of food, our trimark bill is going to soar, and we don't have nearly enough staff to provide the top-notch service that we aim for and that people rightfully expect.

But then, above it all, rises the sounds of happiness: the

laughter of two best friends; the flirtatious banter of a newly met couple engaging in a subtle mating dance over their drinks; the rattle of the bartender shaking and chilling straight-up martinis as Norah Jones croons, "Come Away with Me." This is the score of restaurant life, of my life—the sound of connection, of pleasure, and of possibility. It's the sound of happiness, and no one but those of us working behind the scenes knows that the evening is not going smoothly. Whatever goes wrong tonight, I must not lose sight of the fact that being overrun by happy people is the best problem I could have. It means people trust that if they come to my restaurant, I will take care of them. My team and I will get through tonight, we'll watch each other's backs, and we'll take notes. And next year, if we're lucky enough to face the same problem, we will be better prepared.

A restaurateur sets the scene where people's lives can unfold. In an era when so many people exist in a self-contained bubble, their heads bent down over their phones, their eyes fixed on a screen, I feel blessed to be able to create businesses where the whole point is to drive face-to-face human interaction and connection. Food is the universal link, the unifier that subtly draws all those individual vignettes together to coalesce into one great human narrative. After all, everyone has to eat. For those of us who have made it our business to serve, getting a front-row seat to the happiness that ensues when people feel cared for and well fed, and knowing that we are in some way responsible . . . well, there's not much more magical than that.

Serving up happiness is a great way to make a living, and it's what I live for. How did I get so lucky that I get to do that on a daily basis, and at such a large scale? Well, that's the story of my life.

Two

Eating, Family Style

The only time I have ever turned down a slice of cheesecake was on my twelfth birthday. It was the night I saw the musical *Hair* on Broadway. My mother loved the theater, and every year around my birthday we would go to New York City and see a show, then walk over to Lindy's on Fifty-Second Street for cheesecake. Lindy's was famous for it, a massive, thick, cream cheese–based concoction hugged in a graham cracker crust, a lot like my grandmother Kitty's, for whom I was named and whose recipe lay tucked in her much-treasured recipe box, which contained the only clues I had about a woman who died years before I was born. Kitty's cake was better. It wasn't as sweet, as it was made with dense farmer's cheese, nor was it topped with strawberries drowning in a glossy, goopy, impossibly red glaze.

Grandma Kitty's Cheesecake

Serves 10

32 ounces cream cheese
6 ounces farmer's cheese

1 cup sugar
5 whole eggs
2 egg yolks
5 ounces heavy cream
1 teaspoon vanilla extract (generous teaspoons!)
½ teaspoon salt

Graham Cracker Crust
In a bowl combine:

2 cups of graham cracker crumbs
¼ cup of brown sugar
1 teaspoon cinnamon
¾ stick of melted butter

Press crumbs evenly on the bottom and sides of the springform pan.

1. Preheat oven to 400 degrees. Using paddle attachment, beat cream cheese in an electric mixer until smooth, no lumps. Add farmer's cheese a little at a time—it may look chunky.
3. Add sugar and mix until combined.
4. Add eggs one by one, scraping sides of bowl in between.
5. While mixer is spinning on low, add heavy cream in a slow, steady stream, then add vanilla and salt.
6. Spread batter into a well-sprayed and crumbed 12-by 3-inch high springform pan and bake for 15 minutes. Reduce heat to 300 degrees and bake another 40 minutes. Rotate pan and bake for another 30 minutes, until cheesecake is set.
7. Turn off oven and allow cheesecake to sit for another 20 to 30 minutes. Cool at room temperature and chill in refrigerator.

———————

That night, our seats at the Biltmore Theatre were front and center, best in the house, and I sat riveted as Ben Vereen, Melba Moore, and Diane Keaton belted out the story of Claude Bukowski and his hippie tribe. The play rocked with provocative themes and searing lyrics about sex and drugs, and railed against the draft and Vietnam to pounding, joyous, heartbreaking music that made me think the freedom of my eighteenth birthday couldn't come fast enough. In the course of two hours, my world leaped from *Leave It to Beaver* into the Age of Aquarius. Although I was a worldly and precocious twelve-year-old, nothing could have prepared me for the end of the first act. My mouth dropped open as the entire cast defiantly dropped their clothes. From the first row, I could see everything. When confronted by the sight of my first ten penises, I slowly raised my playbill to cover my eyes.

When my mother and I left the theater and headed over to Lindy's, for the first time in my life, I couldn't eat the cheesecake. That night, this sassy twelve-year-old girl was rendered humbled, speechless, and without appetite. To this day, one bite of a New York–style cheesecake and I'm twelve years old again, on the brink of becoming a young woman and a little scared to see what's ahead.

Food is memory, transporting us back in time to reconnect us with places we've been, with people long gone, evoking moments we wish to relive and marking the turning points of our lives. Baked goods often seem to be the most powerful evocators, perhaps because good pastry and bread take so much care and effort to make and are so often the accompaniment, if not the centerpiece, of celebrations, gatherings, and special occasions. I couldn't say what I looked forward to more on those ritual birthday evenings out on the town with my glamorous mother, the show or the delectable cheesecake that would follow.

Other dessert-inspired memories take me back to when

I was four or five, walking back to Nana's house in Nantasket after spending an afternoon at the beach, the smell of the beautiful babka or pies she had set to cool on the windowsill wafting out to greet us in the salt air. While the grownups socialized and sipped cocktails in the backyard before moving to the big front porch for dinner, I'd gaze longingly at the dessert, trying to calculate how big a slice I'd get given the number of aunts, uncles, and cousins with whom I'd have to share.

Jewish comfort food is generally time- and labor-intensive, which surely explains why Dora, my maternal grandmother, spent most of her days in the kitchen, especially when our extended clan descended upon the house she shared with my grandfather, Barney. And the kitchen was where I could often be found—if I wasn't at Paragon Park, in town at Weiner's bakery eating rugarts, or on the beach—sitting at my grandmother's feet, trying to stay out of the way while watching her magical hands work and shape our food, whether into little sweet and sour meatballs, stuffed kreplach redolent of ground beef, delicate cheese blintzes, or light-as-air matzo balls ready to plop into fragrant, parsley-flecked chicken soup. Nana didn't have much patience for questions, but she would let me help as long as I followed her instructions exactly. She taught me that technique is important. The baking process particularly fascinated me, how something could go into the oven looking so bland and raw, only to come out regally puffed up, golden brown, elegant, grand, and delicious.

Nana Dora's Passover Matzo Meal Puffs

Serves 8

    1 cup vegetable oil, to fill muffin tin
    2 cups matzo meal

  1 ½ teaspoons salt
  2 teaspoons sugar
  2 ⅓ cups water
  1 cup oil (50/50 mix of olive oil and vegetable oil)
  6 large eggs

1. Preheat oven to 400 degrees.
2. Mix matzo meal with salt and sugar. Whisk in water and the oil mixture.
3. In a saucepan, bring matzo meal mixture to a boil. Remove from heat and whisk in 1 egg at a time.
4. Place medium-size muffin tin on a cookie sheet and place in the oven. Preheat tin coated with vegetable oil 5 minutes.
5. While the mix is still warm, fill muffin tins to the top with the matzo meal mixture, being very careful of the hot oil in the tins.
6. Bake for 20 minutes, or until the batter is lightly golden brown and puffed up.

Nana Dora's Matzo Balls and Chicken Soup

Makes 12

  4 large eggs
  2 tablespoons chicken fat
  ¼ cup seltzer
  1 cup matzo meal
  Salt and pepper, to taste
  Chicken soup (recipe follows)

1. Mix together eggs, chicken fat, seltzer, matzo meal, and salt and pepper. Refrigerate mixture for 3 hours.

2. Dipping hands in cold water, form 12 balls.
3. Bring chicken soup to a boil and place matzo balls in soup.
4. Cover and cook for 30 minutes, until matzo balls are soft.

Chicken Soup

Serves 8-10

    6 quarts water
    2 large roasting chickens, approximately 5 pounds
    3 whole onions
    4 parsnips, unpeeled and halved
    1 package celery with leaves, coarsely chopped
    6 carrots, peeled and left whole
    1 large sweet potato, cubed
    Parsley
    Kosher salt and peppercorns

1. Put chicken and water in a large 16-20 quart stockpot and bring to a boil. Skim off the froth and lower the heat to a simmer until the vegetables are roasted.
2. Place onions, parsnips, celery, carrots, and sweet potato on a baking sheet and roast in a 350-400-degree oven until just brown.
3. Add all the roasted vegetables to the stockpot with the chicken and liquid. Simmer for 3 to 4 hours until the chicken starts to fall off of the bone.
4. Refrigerate. Skim fat from the soup. If you want to serve it without the bones, strain and pick chicken when cooled, then put the meat back in the soup. Reheat and serve. Add

chopped parsley to brighten the soup prior to serving. Add one matzo ball per soup serving.

My grandmother's artistry was especially meaningful to me because I so rarely saw my own mother in the kitchen. My mother, Barbara, was raised in modest circumstances in Mattapan, across the street from a mental asylum, or as she called it, "the nut house." The youngest of three by six years, Barbara's trajectory changed from that of her siblings when her parents shipped her off to a boarding school in New Jersey at a young age. While there she got a glimpse of a whole other world that she didn't know existed. As Mom tells it, the day she visited her good friend's family at their lovely country home in Connecticut was life changing. The house was classic and traditional, with large airy rooms and beautiful gardens. Her friend's mother belonged to a garden club and breakfasted in the garden room, where she was served with pristine crystal and silver. Mom had never seen such an upper-class, cultured life except in the movies, but once she knew it really existed, she formulated a vision for the life she wanted to create one day for her family and kids. For me.

Fiercely intelligent and ambitious, Barbara grew up with high hopes for herself. Stunningly beautiful, with a degree in comparative literature, she used her considerable artistic talents and exquisite taste to become one of the area's most visible and influential corporate wives, as her husband, my father, parlayed his natural business and marketing acumen into a career as one of the most powerful financial players in Boston.

The story of my parents' rise to local prominence began when Dad's father, Sam, a well-respected obstetrician, dropped dead of a heart attack at the age of fifty after eating a huge dinner at Mama Leone's in Manhattan's theater district. Until then, my dad had hoped to follow in his father's footsteps and become a doctor, but his application to medical school was turned down. So he went to work for my mother's father in his furniture store, where my dad learned about business in general, the ins and outs of payables and receivables, and discovered that he was quite talented at keeping the books.

As an inheritance, my twenty-two-year-old father and his young wife, my mother, were left with a box of old IOUs. Having accumulated some wealth over his medical career, my paternal grandfather had been exceedingly generous and made many loans to people in the community. Following his death, my father had to collect all the debt that was owed, going door to door to the baker, the taxicab driver, the butcher, and all the other local businessmen to whom my grandfather had loaned his money. He was able to recoup most of the money, just over $100,000, and this became his and my mother's nest egg. He continued to collect interest on the loans he couldn't recover, with the exception of the one belonging to the debtor who met him flanked by two of his goons and pummeled him in the back room of a dry cleaner. He wrote that loan off. In the end, collecting the money became the genesis of my father's long career as a lender.

He opened his own lending company, JSA Associates, on Devonshire Street in downtown Boston. Being a commercial lender was a bit like playing the Wizard of Oz, doling out the gifts people needed to achieve their dreams. As my father was always extremely astute about those he loaned money to—he loaned to the individual, not to the business—he was rarely met with a default, and the business thrived.

But when banks started going into commercial lending themselves, my dad became their competition, and in 1959, out of the blue, his credit line was shrunk by half. Stung, he decided that to prevent such a thing from ever happening again, he would simply buy his own bank. He got the money he needed through a group of investors who loaned him money, as well as from my mother, who sold her diamond engagement ring to help, and bought the Brighton Bank and Trust Co. Brighton wasn't a neighborhood you particularly wanted to advertise, so Dad wisely renamed his bank the much more prestigious sounding Barclay Bank and Trust, and my mother worked her magic on the interior, dressing it in British style décor. As a leader for several charities and fundraisers, she had access to a large list of wealthy, educated women who were excellent potential clients for the bank, so Dad developed a monthly series called Brunching with Barclay to give women a chance to hear important and interesting accomplished professionals speak. The program gave Barclay's a touch of class and gravitas, and it gave clients a reason to come to the bank. To polish the bank's image even further, he sent out his deliveries in a fleet of old-fashioned British livery cabs. When the original Barclay's Bank in London threatened to sue, he changed the name to Barclay Bank of Boston, but by then he had already started to acquire other local banks. He bought the bank across the street from his, and to bring attention to the banks, he painted the white parameters of a tennis court on Court Street and strung a tennis net between the two buildings. He then announced the merger with an ad campaign that hinged on the notion of friendly competition.

Whenever I'm trying to come up with creative marketing initiatives for my restaurants, I try to channel a bit of my dad's showmanship. I got my marketing genes from him, no question. That's why I did so well producing commercials in the advertising world. I thought I was making little sixty-second films, but in reality I was honing my ability to understand a brand, market it, and sell it. In any retail business, your marketing determines how people see you. That's why my father renamed his banks, why he put a tennis court in the middle of the street, and why he invited prestigious Boston businessmen to speak to his clients.

Marketing is all about sending messages. It's why any time the temperature rises above eighty degrees in Boston, you can come to my restaurant MET Back Bay and find us doling out free push-up pops in flavors like roasted pineapple and chili or whipped cappuccino. The message is: we know hospitality, we give you treats on the house! Such a marketing move is also a way to reinforce the fact that we're modern and creative. We sell a lot of hamburgers and steak, but we can do other things and we're going to let you try it for free. It's a moment when we can show our playful side, and that's fun. When we put free popcorn on the bar in Chestnut Hill, we're again showing our hospitality, but we're also saying, "Thanks for coming in."

We sent another message when we launched our day-of-the-week specials. The economy had taken a turn for the worse and we needed to emphasize that; though we were elegant, we were affordable, too. So we started serving specials like Monday burgers, Tuesday tacos, and Wednesday two-for-one lobster. They've been so popular that, even now that business has improved, we've kept running the promotion. We highlighted our global sophistication when we decided to introduce a lunch menu presenting round-the-world salads—on Monday, you could eat in Rome, Tuesday in Paris, Wednesday in Barcelona. And when we started serving brunch, we heralded the move by announcing the creation of the Egg MET Muffin, a decadent and high-end version of the McDonald's classic. Great marketing is all about targeting your audience. Figure out what they want, tell them you've got it, and sell it to them.

English Muffins

Makes 27 muffins

> 4 ounces fresh yeast
> 1½ quarts warm milk
> 3 tablespoons sugar

3 cups hi-gluten flour
3 tablespoons salt

1. Bloom yeast with milk and sugar.
2. Add flour and salt, mix with paddle for 5 minutes.
3. Cover and allow to rise until tripled in volume.
4. Spray parchment lined sheet pan and sprinkle heavily with cornmeal.
5. Line rings with silica paper (paper should not be higher than the ring).
6. Using a # 10 scoop, portion batter into ring mold.
7. Proof for approximately 20 minutes in alto sham or until doubled in size.
8. Spray second sheet of parchment and sprinkle with corn meal.
9. Lay on top of muffins.
10. Cover with flat sheetpan.
11. Bake at 325 degree convection for 15 minutes, spin, and bake for an additional 15 minutes.

My father understood this well, and his business grew. Then one day in 1971 he found out about the availability of another bank, the United States Trust Company of Boston. The Morse family had owned the bank for many years, but because the Morses couldn't choose a successor from their family without creating ill will, they decided to sell. Dad was dogged in his attempt to buy this bank. He was just short the full sum he needed, so he embarked on a series of meetings with a banker who was willing to loan him the cash. Knowing this particular banker had a habit of drinking three or four martinis at lunch, my father would drink a quart of milk before every meeting to make sure he could keep his wits about him while they negotiated. He got a good chunk of the money, but he needed several million more to close the deal. The Morse family wanted all bids in to them by week's end, and the clock was ticking.

My dad tracked down Clark Coggeshell, a well-known banker from the Chase Manhattan Bank, who was vacationing in Miami Beach. My dad and my mom hopped on a flight to Florida, Mom's itsy-bitsy bikini stashed in her bag, and proceeded to negotiate their future with Mr. Coggeshell and his wife in a poolside cabana at the Fountainbleu Hotel. At the end of two days my father walked away with the money he needed to put his hat in the ring for U.S. Trust. It is family folklore that it was Mom's Pucci bikini that sealed the deal.

The Morse family voted and chose to sell the bank to my dad. It was a huge moment in my father's life, and a turning point for our family. Fortuitously, my father had launched his business in tandem with the go-go growth of the seventies and eighties, and we would all be the beneficiaries of his amazing timing and my parents' ability to see an opportunity and make the most of it. With five restaurants under my belt in seven years, I think it's clear I learned by their example.

I'm not sure my parents ever saw themselves as such, but they were great business partners. Both had extraordinarily high standards of excellence, and both had a strong work ethic. He was a go-getter, and knew how to make things happen. Although my mom didn't work at the time, she took her job as woman-behind-the-man extremely seriously. As my father's business grew, Mom worked hard to make sure that our family lived up to the visions she had for us. Getting the right exposure was important to her, as was the reputation of our family name in the community. She was determined not to have ordinary kids, an ordinary house, or an ordinary life, and she took steps to set the appropriate scene and ensure that we would rise to her high standards.

It was she who insisted on moving us out of our dollhouse-sized ranch house to a gorgeous old Georgian on top of the highest hill in Newton. In an era when people were ripping out wainscoting and crown molding to comply with a more contemporary aesthetic, she bucked the trend and revived that aged beauty into a glorious new version of itself. The only nod to modernity was the state-of-the-art kitchen she and my father installed, complete with a gas-ignited charcoal grill. This was a kitchen that could have been plucked from the GE exhibit at the World's Fair—blenders that slid into place on carved grooves on the countertop, mixers that flipped up when in use, cutting boards that seamlessly disappeared into the countertop, and double restaurant-sized ovens. The kitchen was undoubtedly the first of its kind in the neighborhood, and I thought it was the coolest thing I had ever seen.

My mother designed the big house to be an elegant venue for the many business and social receptions for which she would become famous. One of my strongest memories of my mother is of her sprawled on her bed thumbing through Craig Claiborne's *New York Times* cookbooks as she planned yet another of her impressive dinner parties. The books had menu suggestions in the back, recommendations for every possible kind of party, and it was there that my imagination took flight. I would look through those books long after my mother was done making her selections—usually something classically French—marveling at the intricate recipes that represented hours of toil.

Not that my mother would be doing the cooking for these parties. My mother did not cook, with the exception of a decadent batch of one-pan brownies and something she called snowflake cake that had the light, spongy texture of angel food. She carefully and lovingly planned gorgeous birthday parties for my sister and me—for my sweet sixteen, she had a man come to the house to prepare individual omelettes for each of my thirty friends—but our birthday cakes were not made from scratch by a maternal Donna Reed look-alike in an apron. Like everything my mother served, however, the cakes were exquisite—scrumptious, sugar-iced works of art bought from the high-end grocer S.S. Pierce. My mother was not interested in cooking, but she always knew where to get the best food. Lucky for us, the best food in our house wasn't reserved for special occasions. Even the chocolate that smeared my hands and mouth while I watched early morning cartoons before everyone else woke up was the best money could buy.

Mom's One-Pan Brownies

Serves 8

You can mix this directly in an 8-by-8-inch baking pan.

> ¾ cup toasted walnuts
> ½ cup butter
> 4 ounces unsweetened Baker's chocolate
> ¾ cup flour
> ¼ teaspoon baking powder
> 1 cup sugar
> 1 teaspoon vanilla
> 2 jumbo eggs

1. In a 350 degree oven toast walnuts until crisp, about 10 minutes. When you start to smell a deep, nutty aroma, pull them out.
2. Melt the butter and Baker's chocolate right in the pan.
3. Mix together the flour, baking powder, vanilla, sugar, and eggs.
4. Add mix to butter and chocolate mixture in the pan. Fold in cooled walnuts.
5. Bake in a 350-degree oven for 25 minutes. Slightly undercook.

When it came to her soirees, Mom expected perfection, and the chefs brought in to execute her dinner parties received strict and exacting instructions as to where to make their purchases and how to prepare the dishes she had chosen. When guests arrived at our home, they'd find a table set for royalty, every dish, wine glass, napkin, and serving piece chosen with great care, glinting in the mellow light set at the perfect level to flatter the women in their glamorous, Sinatra-era makeup and mink stoles. The effect upon walking into the dining room was nothing short of breathtaking.

My mother applied the same imagination and refined aesthetic to all of her volunteer work, planning and decorating countless luncheons, big hospital fundraisers, and charity balls. I spent many hours of my youth stuffing envelopes, crafting centerpieces, and planning menus with her for these events. Thanks to her instruction, I can create a fabulous cheese display in five minutes using a few ordinary containers found around a typical kitchen. She had an incredible aesthetic sense, and could take any random thing and turn it into something beautiful. Mom hated to cook and was happy to pay others to do it, but she was the original design and décor do-it-yourselfer. Her parties and fundraisers were spectacular as a result of her hands-on attention to quality, presentation, and detail, but the real key to the success of those gorgeous evenings was not the glitter that adorned the table, it was Mom's irrepressible generosity. I like to think that I inherited that quality from her. She loved putting on these parties and watching people enjoy themselves, a fact that stuck with me and has greatly influenced my approach to entertaining and hospitality. Quite simply, a good restaurateur has to love making people happy. The restaurant business is not the right place for anyone who doesn't have a generous spirit.

Though our home was beautiful and luxurious, it could be rather antiseptic. My parents, although loving, were strict, serious people preoccupied with getting ahead, highly concerned with appearances and decorum, and difficult to please. They had a lot of rules. Humor wasn't their strong suit. For levity, when I wasn't creating my own distractions by tap dancing on the table or, when I was older, sneaking out of my bedroom window in defiance of yet another grounding for who knows what infraction—I'd escape to the kitchen to hang out with Lulu, our housekeeper, cook, and resident philosopher.

Lulu had come to work at our house when she was sixteen, though my mother thought she was twenty-one. She had a lot of warmth and heart—just what the house was missing. She executed Mom's instructions perfectly, down to sitting my sister and I at a play table for days on end to drill us on our table manners, but when all that was done we would sneak into her room to listen to Motown records. She would teach us the shimmy while listening to the likes of Aaron Neville singing "Tell It Like It Is." I was nine years old.

Early on she taught me about courage, insisting that I learn to defend myself and never let anyone put me down. She could spot a true friend from miles away and taught me to be discerning when it came to the people I chose to let into my life. And of course, she recognized the bad boys as soon as they showed up on the horizon and made no bones about trying to steer us clear of them. She would always say, "Kathy Grace, now, mind your Ps and Qs," meaning, stay out of trouble, girl. Because she knew I was attracted to trouble. Yet while she was smart enough to appease my mother, she also knew enough to allow us girls the freedom we needed in order to grow up. She loved her gossip, but you could trust her with your life. For all of these reasons and more, I adored Lulu. And of course, Lulu could cook.

I was at her side nightly while she cooked up batches of food that harkened back to her Southern roots in Alabama, like crispy fried chicken, biscuits, and salmon croquettes. She perfected Swedish pancakes, a favorite of my mom's, and it became a Sunday morning staple. As always, where there was food, there was comfort, and it was through Lulu's influence and patient instruction that I intuited the difference between a cook and a chef, and which one I was destined to be. Lulu would stay with our family for close to eighteen years, until my sister got married at twenty-one.

Lulu's Buttermilk Biscuits

24 Biscuits

8 cups flour
2 tablespoons plus 2 teaspoons baking powder
2 ¼ teaspoons baking soda
2 tablespoons salt
¼ cup sugar
16 ounces frozen butter
1 quart buttermilk

Combine everything but buttermilk and mix until butter is "pea sized." Add buttermilk and mix until combined. Press out onto floured table, fold several times, and roll out and cut. Arrange on pan very close together and brush with butter, bake at 400 degrees until golden brown on top. When the biscuits are hot, brush melted butter on top.

I'd also escape to my oldest best friend Cindy Swiman's house for a dose of normalcy. Cindy's family was not wealthy, but Cindy taught me that friendship and human connections were far more valuable than anything money could buy. Her mother was a Jewish Betty Crocker, a quintessential, traditional, Middle American housewife, ten years older than my mom and her total opposite. On the surface she seemed perfectly ordinary but she was incredibly special—so warm and welcoming. There was always a freshly baked cake on display in a cake box with a Lucite hood on the left-hand side of her kitchen counter so that anyone who walked in the door could see it. There was one to die for made from a cake mix but doctored up with instant vanilla pudding and chocolate chips, but my favorite was her sinfully rich sour cream coffee cake. You could just taste the love in there. When Cindy grew older and started baking the cake herself, her mother would always ask, "How do you get it so fluffy?" Cindy would reply, "Mamala, I made it with love, just like you did." Her mother didn't remember that her own cakes were gorgeously fluffy, too.

Doris Swiman's Sour Cream Coffee Cake

Serves 8

½ pound butter (softened)
1 cup sugar
2 eggs
2 cups flour
1 cup sour cream
1 teaspoon vanilla
1 teaspoon baking powder
1 teaspoon baking soda
Cinnamon and sugar, mixed (¾ cup to 1 cup)
¾ to 1 cup chopped walnuts

1. Preheat oven to 350 degrees.
2. Grease—or spray with cooking spray—a tube pan, preferably nonstick, with a removable bottom.
3. Cream together sugar and softened butter and vanilla in a bowl with a hand mixer until really smooth, 2 to 3 minutes.

Add eggs to mixture—one at a time—beating with hand mixer all the time.

4. Alternate adding flour, baking powder, baking soda and sour cream, and continue to mix until done. (I usually do 3 rounds of each.)

5. Pour half the mixture into the prepared pan and spread with spatula. Smooth around til even. Generously sprinkle half the sugar and cinnamon mixture on top, then sprinkle with half the chopped walnuts. Pour rest of batter on, and spread til even. Sprinkle with rest of sugar and cinnamon, then walnuts.

6. Test the cake for doneness after 20 minutes or so. It should be done by 30 minutes, when golden brown on top.

———————

Like mine, Cindy's family entertained a lot, but the gatherings were usually cheery informal preludes to their Saturday nights out, hanging out with their best friends in the den, drinking cocktails with Wispride port wine cheese spread and crackers. Today, in honor of Cindy's mom, my guests are welcomed with a big scoop of Wispride and a clutch of sesame sticks when they come into my restaurant MET Back Bay. I may run a big business and big restaurants, but I try to incorporate my heart and soul and a personal touch at every level that I can. It's those kinds of details that can help a restaurateur differentiate the business and keep it from feeling soulless and corporate.

There were other women who were hugely influential, close girlfriends of my mother's who were all aunties to me and showed me the vastly different ways women could lead their lives. There was Auntie Betty, who was my very own Auntie Mame with her tremendous personality and the long line of men at her feet. There was stylish Auntie Ryna, who was divorced young, remained childless, and was intent on never marrying again. Sydele, who passed along her obsession with blue and white china to Stephi and me. The Schusters and the Millers were our closest family friends and the cadence of normalcy in our lives. In my family we rarely had sit-down weekday family dinners, but you could count on finding a pot roast or a brisket on the table precisely at 6 P.M. at either Elaine's or Lorraine's house nightly. It was Lorraine who insisted I put a tuna sandwich and an omelet on the Chestnut Hill lunch menu. "People like to eat plain good food," she said. And she was right. Mom kept very few pastries in the house, but Elaine had a corner in her kitchen that would rival any bakery, stocked with frosted cupcakes, mile-high cakes, freshly bought pies, and assorted cookies. There was even a candy drawer. She liked her sweets. I adored being at their house in the thick of the action with her fun-loving husband, Gerry, who never passed up the chance to play a good prank, her three sons—Mark, Todd, and Scott—and her daughter, Jody. Scott, her middle son, grew up to be a much-cherished advisor in my life and business. The decision to build my third restaurant in Dedham was largely instigated by Scott, who correctly saw the opportunity as my ticket to cash flow that would enable all kinds of new business possibilities.

Mom's best friend Ellie Groper lived on our street, literally right down the hill from us. I would climb up and down that hill to and from Ellie's house many times a day, whether it was on the way to school, back down to Ellie's for dinner, or running down the hill after the sound of the ice cream truck bell. Once, on an icy day in the dead of winter, I was late for the bus to Hebrew school and I tumbled down the hill, landing knocked out cold in Ellie's yard. Fortunately, she was looking out her kitchen window, saw me, and rushed me to the hospital where it was determined I had a bad concussion. Thank God for Ellie, she literally and figuratively rescued my sister and me. She was my second mother. It was from Ellie that we learned to laugh. To let it roll. To hang out. To have fun. She taught me that life is a little easier when you have some humor. She also she passed on her addiction to everything chocolate.

In front of Ellie's house and all around the neighborhood the local kids and I spent our childhoods collecting baseball cards, competing to see who could pogo stick or bongo board the longest, running bases, playing four square, and listening to the strange music the older kids in the neighborhood were playing like *In-A-Gadda-Da-Vida* by Iron Butterfly, or Donovan.

As we got older, my sister—focused, disciplined, inclined to follow rules, and content to concentrate on her schoolwork and her intense competitive ice skating training—seemed capable of balancing her own needs while still managing to satisfy our parents' exacting standards. I, a more social, somewhat defiant girl, created many more waves and headaches for them as I chafed against their rules and expectations. Ironically, what they fought so hard to tamp down in me—my stubbornness, my anti-authority streak, my willingness to take risks, and my social butterfly tendencies—were the exact qualities that would give me an advantage in my chosen careers. My strong personality was a double-edged sword, giving me the confidence to easily accept the nomination of camp bunk leader, team captain, or cheerleader (yes, cheerleader), while also getting me kicked out of Beaver Country Day School in the eighth grade for instigating a class mutiny and swearing (in English, unfortunately) at my French teacher, Mme. Jolie. Perhaps my father wouldn't have swatted at my legs quite as severely as I dashed up the stairs just inches away from his belt had he known that my insolence was merely a symptom of strong business leadership abilities that had yet to mature.

My family didn't talk much about our feelings, but through food, we could communicate. Our pastime was eating, and while we were eating, we usually talked about food. Food—finding it, buying it, trying it—was what connected us as a family. Either parent would have been hard pressed to find another partner whose obsession with fine food matched his or her own. My father, in particular, had a complete, unadulterated obsession with it, and because my passion rivaled his own, that was our connection. It may have been our only connection. I was like him in many ways. My hands are his hands. My face is his. And yet, my mercurial, unpredictable, and stubborn nature proved frustrating for him. I did my best to find opportunities to get close to him.

Since neither my mother nor my sister enjoyed sailing or even being on a boat, I developed an interest in sailing so that I could be with my father. He was an avid sailor, and shared a boat with friends for years until he finally bought several of his own. The names of his boats were fitting: the *Brain Trust*, named so because he shared it with his friend Ziggy, who was a shrink; the *Superstar*; and the *Amulet*. I named a drink at MET Back Bay after the *Amulet*. It became my job over the years to provision the boat and to cook lunch in the galley. I would agonize over choosing just the right picnic items or menu for lunch that would please him. I knew to always pack his favorite snacks—roasted almonds and raisins, and Venus wafers and Jarlsberg cheese. He was particular. You dared not board the boat without those items. And you dared not mention lunch before he did. If he was hungry, it was time to eat. If he wasn't—well, too bad. When I was younger he kept his boat in Marblehead, and on the way home we would stop at the Driftwood, which can still be found at the top of the harbor there, and pick up a quart of crispy fried clams and skinny onion rings to happily share in the car on the way home. I still love fried clams.

We nicknamed my dad Captain Bly because he was often so dictatorial on the boat, but on those days when it was just the two of us out on the water, he was at his most approachable. He was never happier than behind the helm of his boat on a broad reach, his Greek sailing cap tipped to one side. Over the years I sailed many places with him: the Abacos, the Grenadines, the Virgin Islands, St. Barts, Nevis, Antigua, up and down the exquisite coast of Maine, and, of course, throughout New England through the Cape Cod Canal to Nantucket and the islands. We would race in Newport every summer and find our way to Shelter Island and the Hamptons. Sailing was a way of life, and he loved it. On shore, our relationship could be strained, but out there on the water, during these moments centered on food and sailing, things felt right between us. As I grew older I became preoccupied with my own interests and social life, and I stopped sailing with him as much. It wouldn't be until I decided to open my own restaurant, long after I had proven myself in the film world and he had already made his mark on the Boston restaurant scene, that we would come anywhere close to recapturing the rapport that we shared when I'd accompany him out on the boat.

Boston in the late 1960s and early '70s, before my father revitalized the restaurant landscape, was a city of two eating extremes, low and high end. Amidst the shiny new McDonald's and casual saloons, there were glamorous hotel dining rooms like the Ritz, famous for their lobster whiskey; and the Copley Plaza's Oak Room, which was a highbrow steak house; and old stalwart lobster houses like the Union Oyster house and Pier Four, which served enormous popovers and lobsters of all sizes; and Jimmy's Harborside, which was Pier Four's competition. You were either a Pier Four family or a Jimmy's family and the two were distinctly different. We were loyal to Pier Four. There were also a handful of luxury restaurants, like Locke-Ober's, founded in 1875, where women were not allowed to dine in the main dining room until 1972; and Joseph's (now the site of my fourth restaurant), which served continental cuisine and potatoes ten ways; and Maison Robert, offering classic French fare and a perfect tarte Tartin. There were a few famous Italian restaurants in the North End, like

Stella's, where their adept maitre'd flambéed shrimp scampi and made Caesar salad tableside. In all of these restaurants, the mood was sedate and the presentation was formal. It was a different era all together. You could find my parents at one of these establishments almost every Friday and Saturday evening, and as the years progressed, we would find ourselves eating out as a family at least three or four times a week at one of these iconic restaurants. They became as familiar and comfortable to us as our own dining room.

Typical of every suburban Jewish family I've ever known, we reserved Sunday nights for Chinese food. We'd descend upon Dave Wong's China Sails to meet the Millers and the Schusters. There were usually six parents and nine kids all roughly the same age in our group—we were trouble and it was a great time. There was nothing like China Sails' pork fried rice and shrimp and dark lobster sauce. Occasionally, we'd meet with other friends. If it was the Gropers it meant we headed to Anita Chu's, where the Char Shel Din with huge chunks of roasted pork and crisp roasted almonds was among the best (dark sauce, no MSG, please). With the Gens we would go to Ho Sai Gai, which had the egg rolls and chicken wing appetizers. We ended up calling Ho Sai Gai. Ho Sai Gens because they would never go anywhere else. Sometimes we'd meet my cousins, which meant that we went to Golden Temple, where the doublewide spareribs were legendary (and still are). My cousins Wendy and Karen who live in Palm Beach and Los Angeles still have the famous Golden Temple ribs flown to them on special occasions.

There was a place in Chinatown that was reserved for very special Sunday nights when Dad and his friends wanted to drive their families into town. It was called the House of Roy, and it was a dump. But man, was the food good. My father would eagerly sing out, "Smell that crazy cooking!" as we drove down Tyler Street, and we all would delight in his joy and in the meal to come. The House of Roy had more authentic Chinese food than we got in the burbs. The menu stated, "No rolls, no chop suey, no chow mein—this is a Chinese restaurant." And hence, a delicious shrimp in tomato sauce, and sweet and sour pork that wasn't red like it was in Chestnut Hill, but rather coated with a clear candy-like glaze clinging to the crunchy yet moist pork nuggets. We ordered it without the cherries, just the pineapple. In fact, we customized every dish at our Chinese restaurants. It's how I was raised. I think this speaks to why I don't hesitate to grant my guests any modifications or substitutions they request. I will skin and split and subtract any item or even three from any given dish. I am proud of that. I am eager to please my guests, and I think it pleases people to eat food they like. If you don't like cherries, you shouldn't have to eat them.

For all that we ate out often together, it was on our family vacations, far from the routine of home and the pressure to be perfect, that we were able to participate in rare but precious bonding moments. My mother had serious wanderlust, and we were lucky to be able to travel. She saw travel as a form of education, so my sister and I were frequently taken along on my parents' trips, especially to Europe. One summer when I was thirteen she picked me up from summer school and we traveled together from Geneva to Paris, Capri, Venice, and Saint-Tropez. It was the first vacation where she allowed me to make all the plans, booking the flights, checking into the hotels, and choosing the restaurants where we would eat. I've never stopped making the plans!

It was on that trip to Venice that I made my first visit to Harry's Bar, Hemingway's hangout. We had the famous baked green tagliolini with ham, which Arrigo Cipriani tops with Parmesan and then places under the broiler. We were also given perfect little ham and cheese fingers that are not on the menu. Talk about making you feel special. They were perfectly cooked, with a golden brown crust on the outside and four different cheeses inside. They were served in little wax papers so your hands wouldn't get greasy. The food at Harry's Bar was just extraordinary. We also went to other iconic restaurants like Le Club 55 in Saint-Tropez, L'Ami Louis, where thirty-seven years later I would dine with my closest friends for my fiftieth birthday, and Lasserre in Paris. I loved the copper ashtrays on the table and swiped one, hiding it in my purse. I was mortified when the maitre'd came over and said, "No, no, Mademoiselle, let me get you a clean one." And then he added it to the bill.

My father, often strict and tyrannical at home, was great fun to be around when he could relax and unwind. On a trip to Switzerland he fell so madly in love with Gstaad that he bought a home there, and so we spent many winter breaks skiing in the Swiss Alps. These were not restful vacations, for at dawn each morning we'd hear him clomping through the ski house in his boots, making sure we'd be the first skiers out on the slopes. But the early-morning torture was worth it to bask in his happiness.

After a morning skiing in the fresh *poudre,* as my father called the new snow in his thickly American-accented French, we would meet on the outside deck at one of his favorite ski lodges. Sometimes we went to the top of Eggli, where he claimed they had the best chef, to share some *gemischter salat*— a composed salad of veggies lightly dressed in vinaigrette— and thinly sliced Hoblekase cheese along with a "little taste" of Bolognese. Sometimes we'd go to the Hotel Alpenrose, my personal favorite, where they made the best version of macaroni and cheese in the world—small, smooth ziti-shaped pasta afloat in a rich combination of béchamel laced with raclette, appenzeller, and aged Gruyere the best of all the mountain cheeses—topped with perfectly minced sautéed onions. Or we would land on the terrace at the Golfhotel, which had a splendid buffet and was the spot where you could catch the strongest afternoon spring sun. It was here, as our bodies warmed up, that Dad would announce with a broad smile on his face and a glass of crisp white wine in his hand, "This is a Gstaad day." This was his way of saying life is good, how lucky we are to be here, at this time, together. I lived to hear him say those words.

I would spend my whole life seeking and ultimately gaining my father's approval, but naturally my attention and affections were eventually diverted toward other men, each of whom remains forever linked in my mind to the delectables that were an intrinsic element of our courtship. For someone like me, food and love were inextricably connected. At the age of thirteen, while studying French in Swiss summer school, I fell in love with a beautiful German boy and the apple tart I'd eat twice a day at the local café. I returned home only moderately more fluent in French but a good ten pounds heavier. When I was seventeen my first real boyfriend was Thad, a descendant of passengers on the *Mayflower*. Anyone who dared question his pedigree could have checked the ship's register, framed and proudly mounted on the wall in Thad's grandmother's home. For him, I sat through Thanksgiving dinner at his grandmother's house dressed in costume, a chubby Jewish pilgrim unsuccessfully stifling her laughter during much of the strict reenactment of the original feast. The ceremonial and historical aspect of the meal left a lasting and powerful impression.

It was on Thad's family's summer compound in Rhode Island that I would taste my first freshly laid egg, and it was his mother who would take us to the local farm stand, Walker's, which is still there today, and it was she who taught me to slather a piece of white bread with butter and wrap it around a hot corn cob so that the melted butter coated the kernels. We would have contests to see how many ears each of us could consume.

The summer of my senior year in high school, I lived in Nantucket to be nearer to Thad, who was spending the summer on Martha's Vineyard. There I took my first job, at the Sweet Shop, an adorable ice cream store in the center of town. The counter was high and I was short, so my arms were bruised up and down from throwing myself over the counter to serve scoops of malachite chocolate chip and cream-and-coffee fudge ice cream. By the end of the summer I had only seen Thad once, but I had gained twenty pounds from polishing off the warm fudge that, at the end of the day, I would scrape off the container's sides until they gleamed. I also discovered that, while I enjoyed making money and earning some independence, I especially liked the social aspect of the job, interacting with customers and serving them treats that made them smile.

After Thad there was Derek, who seduced me over bacon-wrapped dates stuffed with roasted almonds, and then André, my French tutor turned lover, an exiled Egyptian Jew raised in Rome who was getting his masters from Harvard and tutoring French for money on the side. I'm sure it was our hours of conversation and storytelling, heads bent over steaming cups of Turkish coffee in any number of Cambridge's cozy coffee shops, that subconsciously planted in me the notion that one day it would be a marvelous thing to create a place where people could gather together to talk, laugh, and share great food.

It would be years before I'd act on the idea inspired by my tête-à-têtes with André and by the multitude of happy moments that punctuated my youth, all of which in some way revolve around a special meal or delightful tidbit. Instead, the first steps I took as I launched myself into adulthood and a career seemed to take me far away from anything having to do with food, except for the catering trucks and craft service always present on a movie set. But as it would turn out, the skills I was about to learn—not just how to tell a story, but how to sell a story—would prove invaluable when I finally made my way back to working with food, my first true love.

Three

Launching a Life

I had to go to France to meet the first person who epitomized everything I wanted to be. When I was twenty I went to Brittany to stay with a French friend named Olivier, whom I had met at UCLA summer film school. His family owned a beautiful captain's house in the center of the spectacular seaside town of Dinard. The first time I walked into their charming home, Olivier's mother was seated at the kitchen table surrounded by all of her grandchildren, intently pitting fresh apricots. Pounds of apricots perfumed the room. She had placed a huge copper pot on the stove, and a large scale dwarfed the kitchen table. Carefully measuring equal parts sugar to apricots, she proceeded to make the best *confiture* I have tasted to date.

Madame Guiton's Apricot Confiture

5 pounds apricots
4½ pounds sugar
1 lemon

WHEN I MET FOOD

Pit and quarter 5 pounds of apricots. Weigh after pitted. (They should weigh about 4 ½ pounds.) Take an equal amount of sugar and place pitted apricots and equal weight in sugar in a heavy bottomed pot. Bring to a boil and stir continuously. Turn down heat and cook over a medium heat until reduced, the apricots will meld into the sugar, roughly 20 minutes. You want the apricots to have some texture so, pull off the stove while apricots still have some shape. Add juice of one lemon. Eat warm on buttered toasted brioche.

———————————

The ease and the confidence with which she cooked reminded me of my grandmother, except Olivier's mother was also a renowned French therapist. By that time my mother had worked in her own interior design company for several years before going back to school and getting her law degree, but she still didn't cook. The only other women I knew who could really cook, my grandmother and Lulu, had no other profession. They were all genius in their own way, but until I met Dr. Guiton I hadn't known a professional woman who could cook brilliantly, and she impressed me deeply. I was at the age when a young woman is poised for flight, and meeting her reassured me that I would somehow be able to create a life where I could balance my dual nature, which thrives equally on competing with people and nurturing them. I spent that summer sitting on the beach among Olivier's mother and all of her topless friends, marveling at their unselfconsciousness, eating the best seafood the icy Atlantic had to offer—dark, knotty little periwinkles that I'd excavate from their shells using tiny pins, and bright, briny oysters that went down my throat in one cold slurp—and looking forward to my future. I was going to make movies.

I had fallen in love with Los Angeles in June of my freshman year in college, when my mother took me on a two-week trip to

California. It was just the two of us—my sister had married the year before and was now living in New York City with her new husband. We started out in San Francisco at the swank Stanford Court, dining in its restaurant, Fournou's Ovens. We roamed the streets of Chinatown, stopping to sample pork buns, and Fisherman's Wharf, shopped in Ghirardelli Square, and bought colorfully embroidered hippie tops in Sausalito. We also went to Berkeley, where we ate at Alice Waters' famed Chez Panisse, which was one of the first restaurants to edge San Francisco onto the verge of a food movement that Boston hadn't seen the likes of yet.

We made our way down the coast along the dramatic Pacific Coast Highway, visiting Carmel and Monterey, before stopping at Disneyland for several days. And then, we hit Los Angeles. In her book *Song Flung Up to Heaven,* Maya Angelou writes: "There is about Los Angeles an air of expectation. Not on the surface, where the atmosphere is lazy, even somnolent, but below the city's sleepy skin, there is a suggestion that something quite delightful might happen and happen soon." That is exactly how I felt, and sure enough, arriving in LA that summer with my mother changed the course of my life.

We ate our way through LA. We lunched on the terrace of the Polo Lounge, where I ate my first chopped salad, the McCarthy, named after a famous billionaire polo player. I felt too cool eating on the Malibu Pier at Alice's Restaurant, named after the Arlo Guthrie song and famous for inventing the B52 cocktail. Mom took me to Casa Cugat on La Cienega, because I had become obsessed with Mexican food after being introduced to it in Vail a few months earlier by a good family friend named Phyllis, who was only a few years older than I and a professional skier. One scoop of smooth, cool cilantro-and-lime-infused guacamole and a taste of an airy, puffy sopapilla drizzled in honey, and I was addicted. Every day and every meal in California was an adventure. My mother always knew the best places to eat, and when she was away from home and the daily routine she was fun and relaxed, and she made me feel special. It was rare to get a glimpse of this side of my mother, and I relished every moment.

While we were in LA, we visited very dear friends of my father's, the Martinsons. Connie had been dad's neighbor on Tappan Street and her husband, Leslie, was a film and TV director most notably known for directing the movie *PT 109*. They were exceptionally generous and made arrangements for us to visit the set and watch a taping of *All in the Family*, which was one of the biggest shows on TV at the time. Being part of the live audience dispelled a bit of the magic for me, but I became fascinated by the behind-the-scenes aspect of TV making. Wheaton College, my all-girls college in Norton, Massachusetts, didn't have a film department where I could learn about camera work and script writing, but as soon as I got back to school I added the next best thing to my English lit curriculum—a second major, in theater.

There are few places that resonate with me the way LA did. I don't know whether it was the fact that I experienced it on a special trip with my mother, or if it was the gorgeous weather and the palm trees, or that it was a magical place where movie stars lived and TV shows were made, or just that it was the opposite of Boston in every way. Regardless, I knew that I would have to find a way to get back to LA, and soon.

There was still one more stop after Los Angeles, and little did I know that it had been my mother's real destination all along. Her motive for taking me to California was so that we could wind up in Carlsbad at the well-known La Costa Resort and Spa, where she hoped I would lose the proverbial freshman fifteen that I had gained during my first year in college. By the time we got there I had packed on another five pounds from eating our way down the California coast. The hedonistic tenor of our superb mother-daughter trip evaporated upon arriving in Carlsbad. Instead, I had my first dubious experience of trying to survive on literally six hundred calories a day. It was torture.

I had been struggling to control my weight for a number of

years. The first time I gave any thought to it I was around thirteen years old, unselfconsciously sitting by the pool eating a big hamburger. As I took a bite, my mother, my cousin, and my sister all called over gaily from their chaise lounges, "Enjoy it, Kathy! It's not going to last for long!" They meant eating whatever I wanted without consequence, of course. And they were right. By the time I was sixteen, hormonal changes, the stress of waging a full-blown teen rebellion against my demanding parents, and an inability to resist a single bite of any of the delicious but rich European fare we enjoyed on our vacations had me up to 116 pounds. My sister, who was three years older, was only 109. And so began my mad love-hate affair with food.

My solution for a while was to stop eating and to start exercising. Overnight I went from being an extemporaneous fun-loving kid to a disciplined young woman seeking control and perfection. I had learned well from my mother, who at the time believed that her power was in her beauty, and who would obsess over the slightest extra ounce until she got rid of it. No one found my behavior unusual until my friend Laura's mother came to visit us at summer school and saw me in my bathing suit, which was too loose. Laura's mother sent an article to my mother about this new disease called anorexia that seemed to disproportionately affect adolescent girls. My mother took me to see a doctor and I regained my health. But then, typical of anorexics, my weight swung up to 140. I was now a junior in high school and had transferred from public to private school in Cambridge. Before, I was attending parties where kids snacked on Cheetos; now I was being served chocolate mousse. It was a whole other world, and a bit overwhelming. The experience taught me how to adapt to any social environment, which is instrumental when part of your job is to make people feel welcome and put them at ease.

I would continue to struggle with my weight, such as when I put on twenty pounds by scraping the leftover fudge from the bins when I worked at the Sweet Shop in Nantucket. What irony that I would decide to pursue a career in food, a career that demands I spend my days concentrating almost exclusively on the one thing I'm supposed to limit.

Food is supposed to make us feel good, and it troubles me that so often it is instead a source of pain. My mother once won a lunch with Julia Child at a silent auction, and she took her good friend Annie, Stephi, and me. Julia was strong and lovely and opinionated. While looking over the menu Annie started to grumble playfully about her weight, and Julia interrupted, her distinctive voice firm: "Don't you ever talk about your weight while you're eating. It spoils everyone's pleasure." She shook her finger back and forth, admonishing us all. She was so right. What a shame that so many women treat food as a guilty pleasure instead of a joyous one.

Annie is the daughter of a French baker, and her natural flair for cooking proves that in some cases good cooking is a genetic gift. Nobody makes a pan sauce or roasts a chicken or makes a madeleine the way she does. And her vinaigrette! For years she refused to give me the recipe but now I know—the secret is the Worcestershire. It's so simple, and so amazingly good.

Annie's Shallot Vinaigrette

Serves 4

You can double or triple the recipe and keep in a jar in the refrigerator. It gets better after one day, so I always make it in advance.

   1 large shallot, minced
   1 large garlic clove, minced

1 large teaspoon good French mustard
2 tablespoons vinegar (I use ½ good wine vinegar, ½ good balsamic)
Kosher salt, to taste, and lots of freshly ground coarse pepper
4 tablespoons oil (I use canola oil)
Few drops Worcestershire sauce

Whisk all ingredients together until thick.

———————————

My deep empathy for women who have a complicated relationship with food greatly affects the way I develop my menus today. I know what it's like to be hungry but hesitant to eat. I understand how it feels to look at a menu and despair when the one option that won't derail your diet is the iceberg-lettuce-and-anemic-tomato side salad. Going out to eat should be fun, not another opportunity to feel deprived because you can't have what everyone else is having, or guilty because you choose to have what everyone else is having. I want people to enjoy themselves when they come to my restaurants—that is, after all, the point of going out to eat—and I've worked hard to develop dishes that ensure that, no matter what they order, everyone will leave my restaurants happy and satiated.

———————————

Kathy's Oil-Free Vinaigrette

Serves 8

⅛ cup Dijon mustard
2 anchovy fillets
¼ cup saba
¼ cup capers

2 garlic cloves, chopped
⅛ cup champagne vinegar
¼ cup balsamic vinegar
1 baby squirt sriracha
⅛ cup lime juice
1 teaspoon salt
6 leaves cilantro
4 shallots, roughly chopped

1. Put all ingredients except cilantro and shallots into a blender and blend on high until mixed.
2. Add shallots and cilantro.

———————

I wouldn't say that I ever knew the feeling of satiety while staying at the La Costa resort, but I did lose weight. I returned from LA twelve pounds lighter but still fantasizing about how I would one day have a career in LA. I started looking for something to occupy me for the rest of the summer, and fortuitously found out about a position as assistant to the director on a play called *The Drunkard,* being staged at the Charles Playhouse in Boston. The producer was my father's friend and client, Stephen Mindich. The interview went well, but at the end, he looked at me severely and said, "If you want to make a good impression, never come to a first interview in jeans." I got the job anyway, and it marked the beginning of a long relationship with a new friend and mentor.

I was one of the youngest people on the crew by far, but I held my own. As anyone who has worked in theater will tell you, there is something special that happens when you're working on a play with a group of talented, hardworking people. You become extraordinarily close in a very short amount of time, like a small family. The cast and crew worked hard and played hard, which was exactly how I liked to operate. I became addicted to the camaraderie, the adrenaline, the sense of fun and creativity, and to the anticipation of the live show. I never got tired of watching from the wings to see how the actors subtly changed their performances every night, often adapting according to the feedback they got from the audience. That's the beauty of live theater, and it's the same thing that makes every night at my restaurants so exciting. No two nights are ever the same. This was a place where I felt I belonged.

Theater became my whole world. The first show I directed in college was *Bye Bye Birdie*. The producer was a girl named Anne Bransford, and we quickly became good friends. Our idea of a great night out started with a great night in. I may have been the fourth woman in my family to attend Wheaton, but I was the first to turn my dorm room into a kitchen. I only had a toaster oven, but it was the Cadillac of toaster ovens, the closest thing you could get to a real oven without actually having one. I had brought in a fridge and lined my shelves with pretty containers that showed off my granolas, nuts, and other snacks I bought from the ultracool grocery store Erewhon. Anne's room was a full-blown bar. We hosted a lot of cocktail parties, with people coming to me for their hors d'oeuvres and then going to her for their drinks. It turned out that everything I had absorbed while watching my mother graciously host her fabulous soirees was equally applicable to ensuring the success of a dorm party for a T-shirt and jeans college crowd (and years later, for a restaurant): greet people warmly, fill their plates generously, and make everyone feel welcome. The art of hospitality knows no bounds, and I had learned from the master.

I went on to direct several more plays in college, but all along my goal was Hollywood, not Broadway. I kept my promise to myself to get back to LA as soon as possible, and the summer of my junior year I left Boston to study film at the UCLA School of Theater, Film, and Television. There I made my first film, a five-minute short loosely based on my friend Lisa Green's short story about Americans in Disneyland. It was a complete mess. I was learning how to operate a camera, but I didn't yet understand the language of film, so though I had beautiful footage I had no idea how to link it together to tell a story visually. I would eventually improve, however, and the knowledge I gained would inform my decisions years later when I would design my restaurant logos and other visuals for my business. Film is a language of visual punctuation. Film school gave me an acute understanding of the power of colors and how they make people feel. It taught me how the slightest shifts in perspective or narrative speed can impact how your audience experiences the story you're trying to tell. After film school I could never take any image at face value again, whether it was a movie, a photograph, or a logo. The visual perspective I gained affects how I arrange food on a plate, how I position listings on the menu, and how I want a graphic to look on marketing materials. I'm constantly telling a visual story, one that begins the second I walk into the space that eventually becomes a restaurant. Spaces can inspire me and inspire concept decisions. From there I start building the equivalent of a set, a backdrop for all the action in the restaurant. In Chestnut Hill I purposely used colors and textures that I thought the residents of the neighborhood would recognize and feel comfortable in, like crocodile and tortoiseshell, and warm leather and tobacco. In MET Back Bay, however, I departed from tradition and painted all the woodwork white, because it's dark and cold nine months out of the year and I wanted people to think of the restaurant as a warm, light-filled refuge. At all times I'm trying to create magic, and I wouldn't have understood how to do it as well with color, texture, and light if I hadn't attended film school.

I returned home to finish my senior year at Wheaton, and a few weeks before I graduated I learned that I had secured a six-week summer internship at an LA film production company, American International Pictures. I spent the remaining weeks at college vacillating between never wanting to leave the cozy confines of my school and chomping at the bit to get to LA to start my internship and my film career. And then something unexpected happened, as it so often does. The night I graduated from college, I decided at the last minute to stop by a party hosted by a friend and her brother. I drank and mingled, and was getting ready to leave when I saw a man approaching me. His name was John, and he always claimed that as I turned to meet him, he thought, "Oh shit, here comes my wife." Though John's sister had been my good friend and partner in crime in eighth grade at the Beaver Country Day School (the school that kicked me out) I had only met him once before and hadn't paid much attention to him. Now he was all grown up, and he was already a great cook. Just a few days after we met he prepared for me a lamb-stuffed artichoke. He could also make a perfect French omelette. He would teach me to appreciate the simplicity and versatility of eggs any time of day, and now my guests can eat them—beautiful soft-curd-scrambled, just-shy-of-hard-boiled, pillowy poached—at any time, day or night, at my fourth restaurant, MET Back Bay. But no over-cooked diner omelettes! I harangue my chefs when I feel their omelettes haven't been consistently worthy of Jacques Pepin.

John was a brilliant, complex, hedonistic guy, bordering on anarchistic. He had been attending Yale but was taking a little time off and working at an architecture firm until classes resumed in the fall. As someone seeking to immerse myself in film, I could not have chosen a better boyfriend. John's father, Alan Trustman, was a famous, award-winning screenwriter who had written *The Thomas Crown Affair*, *Bullitt*, and *They Call Me Mr. Tibbs*. John had grown up immersed in the masculine mythology of Thomas Crown and James Bond, and had something of those characters' irresistibly dashing and sophisticated manner. We were inseparable for a magical three days following my graduation.

I had been living for the day I would fly out to Los Angeles to start my internship, and suddenly I had met this guy who was making it very hard to get on the plane. Thank God for telephones. We must have racked up thousands of dollars in long-distance calls over the following six weeks. He came out to visit me about a month after we met. For one of our first dates, he told me that he was going to take me where they had the most beautiful waitresses in the world. I was excited and tried to imagine to which of the lavish Beverly Hills restaurants he would treat me. The Ritz? Ma Maison? It was neither. He took me to this crazy Mexican restaurant called El Coyote, where all the waitresses looked like their mama's mama. Every time I pass it with my kids, I tell them, "That's where I had my first date with your dad." They never seem impressed, but it was a great night. We spent the rest of our time together traveling up and down the California coast, visiting friends and sailing. Then John left to go back to Yale.

As an intern, I was simply a gopher, but it was a privilege to be in the room. We weren't shooting, just dubbing the movie and doing the sound over. At that time the studio was just wrapping up *The Amityville Horror* and was in the process of redoing the sound for a low-budget, nihilistic, postmodern movie set in a dystopian future starring an unknown Australian actor named Mel Gibson. *Mad Max* was the first feature film for director George Miller, who was making the movie with his friend, producer Byron Kennedy. As a production intern, I was granted access to the studio and got to listen to George and Byron work together. Mel's accent was so thick I could barely understand a word he said. It wouldn't surprise me to learn that he was the reason the whole film was ultimately dubbed, to appease American ears. I would watch the raw footage intently over George and Byron's shoulders from my inconspicuous perch in the corner, but I had no idea what I was looking at. Every day George, Byron, and I would go to this great Mexican restaurant, and I would sit quietly in awe, crunching chips and salsa as they talked. None of us had any idea we had a cult film on our hands that would gross an extraordinary amount of money worldwide and earn multiple awards. The whole experience showed me how sheltered I'd been, that there was a wide world bigger than the one I had come from.

At the end of the summer my internship ended, but I desperately wanted to stay in Los Angeles and start using the contacts I'd made to negotiate my way into another Hollywood job. But John was finishing his degree at Yale and I was equally desperate to be near him. It was a pivotal moment. As strong-willed as I was, deciding on a career in film was really the first decision that I had made completely independently of my parents. Standing up to their disapproval, when at heart their approval was all I ever wanted, had been a major challenge, and having faced it down I felt like I had come into my own and claimed some power over my life. I was looking forward to seeing what I was made of as I forged ahead on my own. Yet here I was, suddenly faced with an unexpected choice—stay in Los Angeles to pursue my career and risk losing John or put off my dreams.

Had we faced the situation today, we might have been able to come up with a creative solution that got us both what we wanted. At the very least, technology would have made a long-distance relationship more palatable. But it was 1979, and there seemed few options. I packed my things and moved back east. My daughter has accused me of making too many decisions based on the men in my life, and maybe I'm guilty as charged. We are, after all, products of the era in which we grew up. But I don't regret my decision. In the end, it only slightly postponed my entry into moviemaking, and it's possible that the experience of abandoning something I wanted so badly made it easier for me to insist that John and I develop a relationship that made room for my goals, and not just his, even if it meant being a little unconventional.

New Haven, where John was studying, was only an hour and a half away from New York City, so I took a job at a small company in Manhattan as a production assistant for a movie called *Michael's Soul,* and moved into my friend Freddie Miller's father's apartment on Fifty-Second Street. I was so happy to be back in New York. I had great memories from the last time I'd been there. When my sister had moved there with her husband, a doctor, she'd lived in an apartment on Seventy-Sixth Street, close to the hospital where he worked. When I arrived for my first visit during my freshman year in college, a sweet yeasty aroma enveloped the building and led the way straight to her apartment. Stephi was baking. Until then the smell of fresh-baked bread had always reminded me of my grandmother Dora and the happy times spent at the seaside in Nantasket. From the moment I arrived on Stephi's doorstep that day, however, it became a smell I associate with my sister. She had become friends with a neighbor who taught her how to make delicious French bread. In one sitting we could devour at least two loaves of this crusty hot French bread, with a wonderfully soft and supple *mie* center, slathered in whipped butter.

Getting to know New York City was fun with Stephi. When she wasn't at work, where she designed children's clothing, she would treat me to the best food the city had to offer: Italian food at Parioli Romanissimo, oversized burgers at Yellow Fingers, and steamed artichokes at Maxwell's Plum. She turned me on to Bell Bates, a health emporium with colorful rows of dried fruit, and a Hungarian store that sold lekvar, a delicious prune butter. Like me, Stephi had an unholy appetite and loved to eat, though she watched her weight carefully and was very thin. Her passion for baking came as a surprise. She hadn't really been interested in learning how to cook until she got married. Once she started making bread, though, she became besotted with cooking and baking. By the time I came back to New York after college, she and her husband had moved to Boston and she'd started taking classes at Madeleine Kamman's world-renowned cooking school, Modern Gourmet.

Living and working in New York (all the while bouncing back and forth between the city and New Haven) did not offer nearly the carefree experience I'd had as a student, but as draining as it was, I loved every minute. I was honored to get to be a part of a film, albeit a terrible one. The person who hired me was a woman named Eva Fyer. During my interview, she asked, "Are you ready to lose your life? Because that's what it takes to be in this business." And I realized that yes, I was.

It was a prophetic question. Nothing could have better prepared me for the restaurant world than my work in film. If you want to achieve recognition in creative, demanding fields like film and food, you have to give yourself over to it, to lose your life to it. You have to be willing to dive in and get swept up in the recurring drama that's inherent in the business. There is no dialing it in if you want to be any good at your art, and restaurant work is as much an art as any other creative field. Like success in film, success in the restaurant industry demands an all-encompassing passion and desire—for the experience, for the challenge, and for the adventure.

Eva was tough, smart, anal, and passionate. And she also loved food. I always believe that people work better when they're well fed—I certainly do—so I was always bringing in great things to keep us going during our long night-work sessions: chopped liver and smoked salmon from Zabar's; dates and nuts from Bell Bates; delicious, creamy coffee ice cream from the Häagen-Dazs shops that were brand new back then and cropping up all over New York City; coffee cakes from Balducci's. The food bonded us, no question, and probably explains what happened next.

You never know what lucky break life is going to throw at you, and in this case, I got to live out the equivalent of every chorus girl's dream. The production coordinator didn't break her leg, but she did leave the film, and I got her job. I had six weeks of experience under my belt while trying to do a job usually held by someone with at least five or six years' experience, and the learning curve was intense. It didn't matter that the movie was bad; I was getting the opportunity of a lifetime, learning the business, the ins and outs of operations, and how to get everything that needs to get done, done every day. It was fantastic.

Then the job was over, and John finished his degree, and in the spring of 1980 we moved back to Boston. We were engaged shortly afterward. John, a computer genius, started working for my father's bank, where he eventually revolutionized the whole computer system, and I took a job as assistant to the editor at *The Boston Phoenix,* once again working for Stephen Mindich, the publisher and my good friend. I was in awe of Stephen, so I was taken aback one day when, in a thoughtful moment, he shared, "No matter how successful you are, you're always still waiting for the moment when someone discovers that you are an imposter." This has stayed with me. Stephen taught me that self doubt isn't necessarily a bad thing. It is humbling. Over the years, as a film producer and as a restaurateur, remembering that even this exceptional man occasionally questioned his merits gave me courage any time I felt fear or self-doubt.

John and I married in January 1981 and traveled to Switzerland for our honeymoon. It made sense. Switzerland had been the site of some of the happiest moments of my life, and I could think of no place I'd rather share with my new husband.

When we weren't cocooned in our chalet, we were on the slopes, wandering the lovely streets, or warming ourselves by the fire at any number of small restaurants typical of the region.

By then I had eaten a number of memorable meals, but nothing, I mean nothing, will ever quite compare to the dinner John and I ate at the Michelin three-star restaurant Girardet, in Crissier. It forever changed the way I saw food and dining. The food was perfection, the service gracious and perfectly orchestrated. I remember the baskets of freshly baked warm breads and rolls that were offered tableside – some toothy with six grains, some salty with pretzel flavor, some studded with fruit and nuts, some plain and perfectly eggy like brioche— all served with hand churned butter and sea salt. There was a game course with whole roasted birds of all kinds – ducks with crisp skin, baby whole pigeon, chicken roasted with the feet and head still on, and birds I hardly recognized. But the pièce de résistance was the cheese course, wheeled out on a large giradon, that was simply startling – five tiers of the finest selection of cheeses you could imagine – creamy, chalky, soft, hard, oozy, Swiss mountain cheese of all kinds – from Tête de Moine to village Raclette, local farm fresh goats, English country blues, French bries, mimolettes and reblochons, Italian parms, fontinas and tallegios – I was in utter heaven. This meal was fit for royalty. It was a king's feast, a celebration of food in abundance and in a fashion I have never experienced since. Not even at Thomas Keller's French Laundry. At the end of the meal, we were invited to see the kitchen. It was shockingly spotless. That should be a restaurant's cardinal rule: clean while you cook.

John and I returned to Boston and continued our respective jobs, but in the spring I applied to Columbia Film School. I was hell-bent on getting a degree in film, and neither my family's disapproval nor my friends' incomprehension was going to stop me. I had never abandoned my dream of making movies, and in a world where labels define you, I was convinced that a degree from Columbia would stamp me with a seal of approval and ensure me the career I wanted. Later, as I watched people with higher pedigrees than mine crash and burn, I'd realize that while labels might get you access and entry, they couldn't compensate for innate stupidity, dysfunction, or amorality. Labels mean nothing. But I was young, and to me, a degree from Columbia meant everything. John couldn't come with me, as his career with my dad was taking off, so in the fall of 1981 I started commuting to New York during the week.

John moved into the attic above the home my sister shared with her husband and two children, and every weekend I'd shuttle up from New York to Boston to be with him. A year earlier Stephi had opened a catering company, Sidell and Sasse, with her friend Bob Sasse, whom she had met when he helped cater a party celebrating my mother's graduation from law school. At the same time, Stephi became executive chef at U.S. Trust, our father's bank. My father was elated that one of his daughters was working in the food business. This was no ordinary corporate canteen. My father wanted to impress his clients, and he and Stephanie designed a state-of-the art restaurant that would have easily held its own if separated from its corporate surroundings. Her work gave her and my father a common bond that I envied.

Every weekend I'd come home to be with John, and inevitably the two of us would wind up in the catering kitchen with Stephi and Bob, helping out wherever we could. Bob was a genius, and he is the reason I know anything about sauces and emulsifications. I was a good instinctive cook, but the techniques Bob and Stephi taught me would elevate my skills tremendously. Little did I know how much I would one day rely on the knowledge I gained in my sister's basement kitchen.

For the time being, however, food was my sister's life, and movies were mine. I gained yet more production experience from a woman named Marion Swaybill. She ran the acquisitions department at WNET, New York's public television station. Though she was about fifteen years older than me, we had a lot in common. Our husbands had the same birthdays and had gone to Yale. She loved theater. She had attended Wheaton. And she was an amazing cook and very much into food. I came in to interview for an internship at the station and we had immediate chemistry. WNET sponsored an independent film festival, and part of my job was to screen all of the submissions and make recommendations. Marion taught me a lot about proper form. We were working at a large company, and I'd never written a memo, had never been in a company meeting, had never thought about how to be analytical and put together convincing presentations. She also gave me a lot of responsibility early on. I even wrote several programming proposals. I walked away from that internship with more work experience than 99 percent of my Columbia classmates, and with a lifelong friend.

Having lived in New York City apartments with their tiny kitchens for most of her life, Marion not only taught me how to handle myself appropriately in the business world, she taught me how to organize a kitchen and clean up after myself. Of all the lessons she imparted, that's the one that I still struggle with, though I'm far better at it than I was before I met her. We spent many holidays together. She had a house in the Hamptons and we would go to Barefoot Contessa and buy hunks of luscious cheeses to serve after dinner, only to finish them up before we started our meal. She got food the way I got food, and she has always remained very dear to me. She and Eva Fyer had a tremendous impact on me and on my career, teaching me as much about food and cooking as about film.

Orzo with Herbs and Pine Nuts

Serves 4 – 6 at dinner, 8 – 10 at a buffet.

Can be served hot, room temperature, or cold and is the perfect accompaniment to roast meat, poultry, and grilled fish.

> 1 pound orzo
> ¾ 1 cup pine nuts
> 1 ½ cups mixed fresh herbs – basil, Italian parsley and chives
> Olive oil
> Sea salt, pepper, and chili flakes to taste

1. Boil the orzo in salted water with a drizzle of olive oil.
2. While the orzo is cooking – or in advance–sauté the pine nuts in olive oil. Watch them carefully as they go from beautifully brown to burnt in a flash.
3. As soon as the pine nuts are brown, turn off the heat. Immediately add the chopped herbs. Stir with a wooden spoon so the nuts and herbs are well integrated.
4. Drain the cooked orzo. Toss with the olive oil, nut / herb mixture. Season to taste with salt, freshly ground pepper and a tiny pinch of chili flakes.

If you are not serving the dish right away, cover with foil and set aside.

––––––––––––––

I went to Columbia wanting to learn how to direct and write, and left two years later ready to be a producer. John and I bought an apartment on Beacon Street, and soon I was pregnant with my first child, Alexandra. It was an exciting time for everyone in my family. My husband was starting to make headway in the financial consulting world, even though he was only midway through completing his MBA at Harvard. Stephi and Bob's catering company was earning a name for itself. My parents had divorced in 1981, and my mother was now an attorney at a firm in Boston. And my father had recently made a business decision that would change not only the trajectory of his banking career but the way Boston, and even much of the United States, would eat for decades to come.

In 1982, two young chefs named Jasper White and Lydia Shire were gaining notice for the innovative dishes they were putting out at the Bostonian Hotel. Jasper was ready to strike out on his own, but at the time there were very few models for chef-owned restaurants. Every bank he approached offered to match his investment in his restaurant dollar for dollar, but as he said in the eulogy at my father's funeral, he "didn't even have the money for a hot dog truck." It wasn't until a friend introduced him to my father that he finally found someone willing to take a chance on him.

Before my parents' divorce, my sister and I and our spouses would go to my parents' home every Friday night for dinner. It was surely there that we first heard my father talk about Jasper for the first time. He spoke about him and his cooking with joyful enthusiasm. When Jasper finally approached my father for help, it wasn't just his extraordinary culinary skills that captured Dad's attention; my father had a sense, a "feel," he said as he rubbed his thumb and middle finger together, that Jasper would elevate the role and title of chef-owner to another level.

Though Jasper had no credit record and had never even had a car loan, after several meetings and several rounds of tough questions, Dad convinced the bank board to loan him the money he needed to open the space he was eyeing on the waterfront. Dad's only caveat was that Jasper work in the kitchen five nights a week until the loan was paid off. Jasper worked in the kitchen six nights per week and paid my father back in three years.

Why was my father willing to go to bat for a chef when no one else in the banking industry would? Quite simply, as a die-hard food lover, he wanted to see more good restaurants in Boston, and Jasper White could cook. And, my dad invested in people, not necessarily in businesses. He was as persnickety about people as he was about food. You had to have the right combination of street smarts and relatability for him to like you and trust you, and once he did, you were in. He just seemed to be able to tell who had, as he would say, the "magic." I think, too, that he saw it as a privilege to be able to help others start a business and create a life. Jasper White's restaurant, Jasper's, featured innovative takes on classic New England cuisine and earned countless accolades, launching Jasper into his role as one of the country's first celebrity chefs.

Simultaneously, it launched my father into the role of Boston's restaurant Oz, the source of the capital that enabled the success many of the area's most prominent chefs and restaurateurs, including Gordon Hamersley and Todd English.

My father's loan to Jasper White also indirectly set the stage for my foray into the restaurant world. For the time being, however, my life was about film, though food still played a starring role.

Four

Life Shifts

The early years following my graduation from film school were magical. John finished up his degree at Harvard Business School, and I gave birth to our first child, Alexandra (Ali). She was six months old when Eva Fyer and her production crew came to Boston to shoot a movie called *Billy Galvin*. Eva asked if I would be interested in being associate production manager, and I jumped at the chance.

When I married, I knew that I would want to start having children early, but I'd also known that I would want to stay in the workforce. When I was a senior in college my mother had transformed herself from dutiful housewife to career woman with a law degree. She had already earned the respect from her community through her fundraising efforts and her interior design work, but until she got that law degree, she didn't feel that she had the credibility or power that she deserved. So she went out and got it. That impressed me, and I, too, wanted to create a career that was wholly mine, not something contingent on what my father or my husband was doing. I had already figured out that the most important thing a woman can do is to become financially autonomous. At the time I thought it was because money gives women power, but now I know better.

Money does give women power, but more importantly, it gives us freedom—to make smart choices, to plan our future, and to create opportunities for ourselves separate and apart from a spouse or partner.

I came of age watching the generation of women before me struggle to find an identity separate from their husbands and far away from their own mothers' kitchens, though, except for the few who were single or divorced, many of my mother's friends—full-time mothers, homemakers, and golf players—remained firmly ensconced in their dependent, domestic bubbles. Some found an outlet in unpaid charity work. My mom, however, took the second-wave feminist message to heart. She wanted more. She went to law school at age forty because she needed to find her voice and wield her own power. She had been my father's closest advisor, his unseen business partner, a major force in helping him build a banking business, but no one acknowledged the importance of her role to his success. Her law degree brought her out from my father's shadow and gave her credibility. In fact, she was asked to join the board of the bank that she had so diligently helped my dad build.

I wasn't going to wait until I was forty for the world to notice me. Gloria Steinem and the women's movement of the seventies and eighties told young women that we could have it all—that it was our right to have it all—and I believed them. I was obsessed with Simone de Beauvior's *The Second Sex*, and envied her unconventional life with Jean Paul Sartre. I had embraced the questions raised by Betty Friedan's *The Feminine Mystique* about establishing the difference between what we wanted and what was expected of us. I thought that being smart and capable and confident would be all I needed to create the ideal life I envisioned when I set out as a young career woman and wife. But as every adult woman knows, the reality is that having it all requires making hard choices, and sometime making painful sacrifices.

My sister, three years my senior, made working mother-hood look easy. She was running her catering company and still executive chef at U.S. Trust, and raising two girls hadn't slowed her down at all. She told me, "Kathy, you just strap the kid on your back and keep moving." So that's what I did.

Billy Galvin was a great experience, and after that I took whatever job I could get—production manager, location scout—on every movie I could. But the reality was that there just weren't that many films being made in Boston, and there was no chance we were leaving any time soon, because straight out of Harvard, John had taken a job at the consulting firm Bain & Company.

Eventually I started to get frustrated by my limited job options. My father had hired an innovative advertising company called Mullen to help him create some good ads for the bank. One of the writers was a supremely talented man named Paul Silverman. When he found out about my writing and film background, he suggested I might be a good fit for Mullen. Commercials? Me? I had gone to film school! I had a degree from Columbia! I was a total snob. But I wanted to work, so I swallowed my pride and agreed to work for Paul on one of my dad's commercials.

Something that has made itself clear to me over the years is that opportunity doesn't make things easy by announcing itself. It doesn't actually knock. Rather, the door of opportunity simply opens, and it's up to you to recognize it and be ready to walk through. When you make something compelling happen from that opportunity, doors continue to open. That is what happened as a result of my decision to work with Paul at Mullen.

The first day I came in to work I met the producer for the ad, Steve Wax. Sometimes you walk into a room and you know that the person you are meeting is about to be someone who is going to matter in your life. Call it kismet. Steve and I instantly liked each other. The very next day, he said to me, "Come into my office, I want to talk to you."

Like me, Steve was passionate about moviemaking, but his experience was far more extensive than mine—he had worked with Francis Coppola and George Lucas. Along the way, however, he had realized that he was better suited to making commercials than feature films, and that he could also make more money in the advertising world. When I met him, he was doing work for Mullen but he had also just opened a new company called Chelsea Pictures. I was interviewing for jobs with WGBH, Boston's public television station, but there was something that intrigued me about what Steve was doing. After knowing me for only one day, Steve asked if I would come work with him at Chelsea Pictures. After knowing him for only one day, I couldn't wait to start.

The advertisement we made with Mullen for my father was smart and hilarious, and to my surprise I had a great time on the project. After that I continued to produce and executive produce other ads, but I did it for Steve and Chelsea Pictures. We were making commercials, but we were hiring feature film directors to direct them. No one else was doing anything like it. We approached each ad as if it were a small, thirty-second movie. We were also the first company to do a series for a campaign, which was considered progressive at the time. Steve and I would conceptualize, write, and pitch together, and we put together an amazing team of people to work with us. In 1987 I became partner. Everything happened so fast. The next thing I knew we had offices in New York and LA, and we'd made many of the commercials that aired during the 1988, 1989, and 1990 Super Bowls.

The experience served as my MBA. Steve was brilliantly creative, but he was an incredibly smart entrepreneur and businessman, too. He taught me everything he knew about how to run a business. Advertising is an extremely visual medium, and though I had honed my naturally strong visual aesthetic in film school, Steve helped me take my skills to another level by introducing me to the Rodchenko school and teaching me how to look at and work with graphics. I use everything I learned from him on a daily basis, and it's because of him that I developed my keen eye for graphic design, and why I am so lovingly hands-on with my graphics and logos, marketing, and branding.

I traveled a lot with Chelsea Pictures, and when we were away on location I was the resident cook because I was a maniac about making sure that there was always great food on the set. I took on the role about three weeks after I started with the company. We were in Belize, shooting just off the coast, on a small island where you could see nothing for 350 degrees but a lone telephone booth we'd had installed for a clever ad we were doing for New England Telephone. We stayed in a dive camp that was made up of little huts and a mess hall. I spent lots of time in the kitchen chatting with the cooks—they made a killer coconut bread that we all devoured for breakfast.

One night, I decided to give them a break and cook for them and our crew. After perusing the kitchen cupboard I realized that, much like the contestants on *Chopped*, I had a limited yet eclectic few items from which to concoct a meal. I settled on a big seafood risotto. Cooking on remote islands forces you to improvise in the kitchen. I cooked the risotto in coconut milk with a local curry mix, more cinnamon than turmeric, and a mélange of sautéed and fried local seafood. The dish was so surprisingly good that the evening's meal took on legendary proportions in our circle and became a much-anticipated tradition. Cooking is alchemy—if you understand technique, you can whip up something marvelous out of nothing. You can make the most exotic locale feel like home. That's really what I was doing on those nights that I cooked for the crew—bringing a little bit of home to a group of people who live more or less like nomads, working insanely long hours while traveling from set to set, from location to location, often leaving family for months at a time. I could think of no better way to thank them than to find a kitchen and get to work.

Seafood Risotto, On-Location Style

Lobster stock:

    8 1½ pound lobsters
    4 cups clam juice
    2 cups white wine
    Cayenne
    Thyme
    Bay leaves
    Salt
    Pepper

Risotto:

    2 cups Arborio rice
    1 cup minced shallots
    4-5 saffron threads
    1 cup dry vermouth
    ½ sweet vermouth

Sauté:

    1 pound shrimp
    1 pound lobster
    1 pound scallops
    knob of softened butter
    ¼-½ cup of cream

Boil lobster in water for 12 minutes. Take all the meat out of shells and reserve—do this over a bowl to catch all the drippings from lobster to add to stock. Roast lobster shells and bodies. In a medium saucepan, add onion and sauté until translucent. Add roasted lobster bodies with shells and cover with clam juice and white wine and the herbs, bring to a simmer and start to reduce. Add salt and pepper. Cook for an hour or so, and then strain.

This will become your basting liquid for your risotto.

In a large saucepan, heat the olive oil. Add the shallots with salt, pepper, a hit of cayenne and cook over moderate heat, stirring, until softened, about 5 minutes. Add the rice and cook for 1 minute, stirring to toast kernels. Crumble the saffron, add it to the rice.

Get the pan very hot and add ½ cup of the dry vermouth. It should sizzle away quickly. Then, turn heat down slightly and slowly ladle the lobster stock—ladle by ladle—adding the juice a ½ cup at a time, and stirring constantly until it is nearly absorbed between additions. Your last ladle should be the sweet vermouth. Add the butter and a hit of cream to finish. The risotto is done when the rice is al dente and suspended in a thick, creamy sauce, about 20-30 minutes total. Season with salt and pepper.

Melt the butter in a large skillet. Add the ¼ cup of shallots and cook over moderate heat until softened, about 2 minutes. Sear the scallops over a high heat to crust the outside and quickly remove and do the same with shrimp and lobster and cook until just heated through. Serve immediately.

It was on that shoot for the New England Telephone commercial that I met another person who would be hugely influential in my film and food life. I was interviewing cinematographers to travel with us to Belize, and an agent, Tom Turley, recommended a man named Robert Richardson. For sure, Bob and I must have known each other in another life. We had a hilarious first conversation and connected on the phone instantly. It's such a small world—he grew up on Cape Cod and we knew several people in common. He had just shot *Platoon* but he was interested in working with Chelsea Pictures when he wasn't shooting films. I flew out to meet him in Los Angeles. I had given birth to my son, Benjamin, only two weeks before, and I was wearing a large sweater to hide the fact that I couldn't button my pants. We met at a restaurant in Century City.

Over the course of a career you'll work with a lot of people, and while some will drive you insane, for the most part you'll get along fine with or without them. But then there are people with whom you experience real chemistry, and when that happens, the result can be magical. I've been incredibly lucky to have more than one person like that in my life—Stephen Mindich, Eva Fyer, Marion Swaybill, Steve Wax. And Bob. There are some people who have an uncanny ability to make you feel like you're the only person in the room; Bob has the ability to make you feel like you are the only person in the universe.

He is very Hollywood in a Cape Cod kind of way, very dramatic, with a shock of white hair falling to his shoulders. Being with him and on the receiving end of his attention can be addictive. The day I met him, he berated me for ordering a tuna fish sandwich. Didn't I know that the tuna industry was decimating dolphin populations with their huge nets? He was as passionate about politics as he was about film. The only thing that might have trumped either was his love for good food and wine. Whether it's the cosmic summer truffle sashimi at Masa or caviar and smoked salmon at Petrossian or Caviar Russe, when Bob loves something he wants as much as he can get, and he wants to share it. We're the same that way. I have shared some of the most memorable meals of my life with Bob over the twenty-five years of friendship that followed that first meeting.

Bob is also the person who has most pushed me creatively. By the time I met him I had already learned that being a producer is mostly about problem solving. That happens to be one of my strengths. For example, one of my first responsibilities when working on *Billy Galvin* was to secure office space for the production company. Unfortunately, they had no budget. But a production manager is a problem solver, so I contacted a friend of Stephen Mindich, Richard Cohen, who owned a large amount of Boston real estate. He showed me some offices in the S.S. Pierce building in Brookline, and as soon as I saw them I knew they'd be perfect. But there was the inconvenient issue of not having any money to pay rent. So I pleaded with him to give them to us for free. He finally acquiesced, and as a thank-you, I sent him a tin of caviar and a bottle of Champagne. The next day, I got a phone call. It was Richard, and he said, "Kathy, I thought you had no money! If I'd known you could afford caviar and Champagne I would be charging you!"

Lesson learned—I had sent him a personal gift, but I should have sent him a gift from the business. That moment crystallized for me the realization that you have to treat your life and your business as two separate entities. If I want to splurge in my personal life, that's a choice I can make. But I don't have that choice if my goal is to run a profitable business. Sometimes I have to catch myself when I'm designing furniture or choosing art for the restaurant and remind myself that I'm not choosing for my home, I'm choosing for the business. It's important to respect the difference between how you can spend on the two.

When I first started working with Bob I felt like I had graduated from problem solving to firefighting. Bob expected me to make the impossible, possible. "Just figure it out, Kathy," he would say. It doesn't matter that you're in the middle of

Jackson Hole and you just traveled three miles to the film site by snowmobile, precariously balancing all of your equipment, only to discover something dropped into the snow along the way. You have to get the shot, so figure it out. Someone forgot a lens in the hotel room. Figure it out. You need to shoot a two-hundred-mile stretch of California coast with angles from the sea, from the air, and from the curving coastline road—and no one thinks to put walkie-talkies in the helicopter before it takes off so that the camera guys up there can coordinate with the guys shooting from the car. Figure it out. Cranes fall, film doesn't get shipped, film gets exposed. The number of things that can go wrong every day on a movie or commercial set are endless, and you spend the vast majority of your time putting out fires and trying to coordinate countless moving parts. And somehow, we always pulled it off. Bob demanded brilliance and excellence. Some days we hated him, but he pushed all of us who worked with him to accomplish more than we ever thought we could. If you're considering a restaurant career, forget the master's degree in hospitality management. Get on a movie set with a genius, occasionally unreasonable madman— it's the best business training you can get. I met Bob early in his career, and it was clear then that he was destined for stardom. He went on to make roughly thirty-five films, collaborating with directors like Oliver Stone, Robert De Niro, Martin Scorsese, and Quentin Tarantino, and garnered three academy awards in cinematography for *JFK*, *The Aviator*, and *Hugo*.

We made a lot of great ads with Chelsea Pictures. Then one day I was shooting an ad for Spalding golf balls in Florida with David Anspaugh, whose most recent credit was *Hoosiers*. Bob and I started horsing around with some clubs and launched a bunch of golf balls as far as we could over a cliff. A few hours later, our client and the ad agency were in a frenzy hunting for the "hero" balls—perfect, color-corrected golf balls that had been reserved for the final product shot. Bob and I looked at each other and realized that we had shot all of them irretrievably into a ravine. Yet another problem to solve, this one of my own creation. But as I stood there staring into the big hole in the ground wondering what I was going to do next, I thought to myself, I don't want to chase hero balls anymore. So in 1995, when Steve decided to move to New York and asked me to move with him, I chose to stay in Boston.

I stopped shooting commercials but stayed on the Chelsea Pictures board and traveled frequently to New York. I started freelancing and producing for friends. Bob and I bought the rights to a terrific book called *Spartina*, by John Casey, and got close to making the movie but never sealed the deal. I also made some music videos with Nine Inch Nails. And finally, I started making movies with Errol Morris, a slightly eccentric documentarian who lived in Cambridge and had done some work with Chelsea Pictures. Coproducing *Fast, Cheap, and Out of Control*—a somewhat surreal 1997 film that explores the blurry line between madness and genius—with Errol, Bob, and Hank Corwin, whose film editing credits at the time included *JFK* and *Natural Born Killers*—was the highlight of my film career.

It was an extremely fruitful time. I have often said that we live life in chapters, and that striking a balance is a matter of shifting priorities before the scale tips too far in any one direction. Balancing life is no easy task when you want it all—to be a successful career woman, an attentive wife, a gracious homemaker, a caring daughter, a loving mother, a close sister, an involved aunt, a trusted friend. Somewhere in there you're supposed to find time to pay attention to yourself, too—to your weight, your health, your head. Anyone who tells you it's easy is lying. I'm not even sure it's possible. Every one of these roles can at times feel like a full-time job, and eventually, trying to do it all can have consequences. Something always seems to get compromised. In my case, at this time, it was my marriage.

When my parents divorced I was twenty-four years old,

and I remember thinking that I would never be dependent on a man the way my mother was. She had held paying jobs, but my father was always the main breadwinner and controlled the purse strings. When my dad packed up his car after thirty years of marriage and left, her world, and my sister's and mine, fell apart for a while. My father shifted his attention to someone else, and we were no longer the priority. Though I was married and had my own family, I felt abandoned and betrayed. My father wasn't the man I thought he was, how could I trust the man I had chosen to be my husband? Everything I thought I knew about what makes marriage work, everything I used as a model for my own relationship, was now suspect. It doesn't matter how old you are when your parents split, it's almost always traumatic, and the timing made me feel incredibly vulnerable. It was painful to learn how easily a person can shift his affection and derail a lifetime of dreams and one's sense of security. My mother wasn't employed at the time and had no money. At least, no money she could access. My parents' finances were tied up in bank stock, and my father ran the bank, so she couldn't touch it. It would take a fierce court battle for her to get back what she had earned. But she fought and eventually won, and in the end she managed her money well enough to become financially better off than my father.

Ironically, fifteen years after my parents' divorce, despite all my vows to never do so, I wound up for a moment in exactly the same predicament as my mother, separated and without access to money.

As much as I enjoyed my work, I had decided that I needed to slow down for a while and make sure I spent enough time with my kids before they flew from the nest. My daughter, Ali, was now thirteen, and I only had a few more years with her and my son, Ben, under my roof. Just as I stopped working, John was offered a job at Aetna in Hartford, Connecticut. He took the job, but I decided not to move with him. I justified my decision by explaining that it was for the kids' sake, that they didn't need to be uprooted. I wanted to keep them near their grandparents. I wanted to be near my family. I wanted to be available should any work opportunity come around that I simply couldn't pass up.

But of course those were just excuses. I think John and I had started falling out of love back when he first started working at Bain & Company. The people who worked there were consulting for some of the most exciting companies in the world, but they were under strict orders not to discuss their work with anyone except other people in their "pod." It made for a strange dual existence for Bain & Company employees, forcing them to live their lives within two entirely distinct spheres. John became wholly consumed by the secretive culture, and I felt like his work became more important than me. Meanwhile, I worked full time for most of our marriage, and as our lives became increasingly independent of each other, John became less and less interesting to me. I felt he was more preoccupied with his business image than anything human and real.

John took an apartment in Hartford and commuted for several months, but soon he started coming home less and less. On his fortieth birthday, March 3, he told me he was in love with someone else. I wasn't surprised. It meant a lot for me to stay in the marriage, but in the end I couldn't. We finally decided to separate in the winter of 1996, while at Stratton Mountain in Vermont staying in a chalet we rented with our best friends, Leslie and her husband Randy. Ironically, the Lamperts gave John a fabulous weekend valise as a fortieth birthday gift. Later the three of us would joke about how they provided John with his walking suitcase.

As chance would have it, about ten years later Leslie's life would eerily parallel mine when she found herself divorced and in the restaurant business. Her marriage split up two days before she was to open her food shop, specializing in soups, called Ladle of Love, named in part, ironically, in honor of the sustenance her marriage provided her. Her restaurant became not only her means to survive financially, but also a way to forge a new identity. Overnight she went from being a wife and mother to being a businesswoman. And she got good at it, fast. She then opened a second business, a farm-to-table bistro called Café of Love, a highly regarded establishment in downtown Mount Kisco, New York.

Leslie's Black Truffle Salsify Soup

2 tablespoons olive oil

3 pounds salsify, peeled and roughly chopped

1 Spanish onion, chopped

1 clove garlic, minced

1 stalk celery, chopped

1 Russet potato, peeled and diced

1 parsnip, peeled and chopped

7 cups vegetarian stock

1 spice sachet (parsley stems, black peppercorns, bay leaf and thyme sprig wrapped in cheesecloth)

3 ounces black truffles, shaved

½ ounce truffle oil

In large stock pot, add oil and heat over medium-high heat. Add onions, parsnip, and celery and sauté for 8 minutes. Add salsify, potatoes, stock and herb sachet. Bring to a boil then reduce heat and simmer for 1 hour. Add truffles. Puree with immersion blender until smooth. Season with salt and pepper and drizzle with truffle oil. Add love and serve.

Regardless of how much I expected the end of my relationship, when it finally happened it came with a profound jolt and sting. I mourned the loss of what we'd once had, the end of our plans for a life and future that would never be.

I was thirty-nine years old, and in light of the divorce, I felt it imperative that I continue staying home with the children. But when John left so did his income, and suddenly our financial stability and my children's future was at stake. The battle for financial control was on, and it lasted years before it was finally resolved. In the meantime, I was suddenly wholly responsible for the kids and myself and our life. I knew I had to earn a living. I thought about moving to Los Angeles to pursue my film career, but the kids were dealing with enough change and I didn't want to disrupt their lives any more than was necessary. Bob and I had always talked about starting a company together, perhaps launching a new beverage product, but that seemed risky at a time like this.

But I came to realize several things about money during this time. Although money gives you freedom, it can also cloud your ability to recognize what's really important in life. I am not saying it isn't lovely to have money—of course it is. But it isn't the answer to happiness. That comes from within—from the satisfaction of getting up every day and challenging yourself to work hard, play hard, and love hard, and from striving to accomplish your goals. Money didn't buy me or my parents love or contentment or the ability to keep our families together. In fact, in many ways having all that wealth weakened us. Yet once all of our dreams were dissolved, it was all that we had left to talk about, or rather fight about. It was tragic. As I fought for what was rightfully mine, I concentrated equally hard on reminding the kids and myself that even if we lost everything, we already had everything we needed.

Survival mode puts everything in perspective. I had always enjoyed simple things but I came to enjoy them even more—a walk around the reservoir, the music on my iPod, a ripe peach, a good book, breakfast with my kids, our ride home from school together, bedtime games of free association. Together we made a lot of magic out of nothing. I made sure the kids saw or spoke to their extended family as much as possible, not just on my side but on John's as well. Trustman, John's sister (who took her last name as her first), and John's mother, Renee, who had always been a devoted grandparent, rallied behind the kids and me. Together we made sure that the children understood that no matter what happened, we were still a family, and to this day I remain extraordinarily grateful for their presence in my life. The divorce was hell, but from it I gained a sense of clarity that I had not had in a long time. Still, I needed to figure out how I was going to pay the bills.

My lifeline came in the form of a kind gesture from my sister. Food is memory and story, and it is comfort. That's why we drown our sorrows in pints of ice cream or slabs of cake—flavors and textures that remind us of good times—when we are sad, sometimes to the detriment of our waistlines. In my case, however, finding comfort in food didn't mean gorging myself to oblivion, though I'm sure I indulged way more than I should have, my thinking being that I deserved to eat well even if my personal life was going to hell. I found a lot of comfort in cooking, and my sister rescued me by generously offering me a job cooking in the food shop of her newly opened restaurant.

Stephi and Bob Sasse had amicably parted ways and closed their catering company, Sidell and Sasse, and Stephi had then opened her own restaurant and food shop in 1994, which she called Stephanie's on Newbury. While she was developing her concept, she and I traveled with her architect to visit all the fancy food shops in Paris, like Fauchon and Hediard, for inspiration. She transformed the old Bookstore Café on the corner of Newbury and Exeter into a tony food shop and lunch spot where people flocked to tuck in to beautifully presented versions of comfort staples like shepherd's pie and meatloaf. Inspired by our childhood trips to Eli Zabar's E.A.T on Madison Avenue, Dean & Deluca on Prince Street in Soho, and the Barefoot Contessa in East Hampton, we made sure the front of the restaurant welcomed guests with a display case brimming with most of the dishes they could eat in the restaurant.

Working in Stephanie's food shop was the best divorce therapy I could have asked for. As sad and angry as I was, it was hard to wallow in those feelings in such a fun environment, especially one that kept me busy from 6:00 a.m., when I came in to get the ovens started, until 2:30 p.m., when I'd leave to pick up my children from school. Stephi and I have always enjoyed cooking together, and side by side we'd whip up enormous quantities of chunky chicken salad with roasted almonds, broccoli with red onion and blue cheese, meatloaf stuffed with Cabot cheddar, quiches of all kinds, and specialty sandwiches. We'd lay them out in the display cases in the front of the restaurant, where they would be ogled by hungry patrons on their way in and packed up to take home for the next day's meal on their way out. I picked up new cooking techniques from Stephi's fantastic prep cooks, some of whom are still working there.

As much as I had heard my father and Stephi talk about their respective businesses, there was still so much I didn't know. But as I did my best to hold my family together—as well as my broken heart—I listened, I watched, and I learned.

Five

It's All About the Bar

The bar is the gateway to a restaurant as well as its heart, the spot where you can feel its pulse, and therefore where you feel most alive. It is somewhat magical in that it can simultaneously serve as a place where people come to be together or to be left alone. It can be the main destination for the night or it can be where the night begins or ends, a place to linger quietly with your thoughts or the short bridge where you toss the stresses of the workday before heading home. With their taps at attention like soldiers in a row and their bottles lined up like small backlit sculptures, bars beckon with the promise of choice and variety. Like no other gathering place, a bar says, "Let me take care of you" and, "Have it your way." Bars make people happy. It was while working at Stephi's food shop that I first witnessed their transformative powers, just one more experience that helped propel me onto a path that I had probably been destined to walk since the day I was born a Sidell.

There was something satisfying about working in Stephi's shop. Not since I'd worked in the Sweet Shop back in Nantucket when I was eighteen, handing out ice cream sundaes covered with hot fudge, had I worked in any sort of retail environment, and I had forgotten the charge I got from witnessing people's immediate pleasure as they enjoyed the results of my work.

I was used to spending months making a movie and then waiting through more months of postproduction work before ever finding out whether the public appreciated the film as much as my filmmaking team and I did. Would the audience get our vision? Would they feel what we hoped they'd feel? There was no way to know until the film premiered. In my new life, Stephi could decide to add almonds to the chicken salad for extra crunch one day, I'd make the adjustment to the recipe the next time I prepared it, and hours later I could see her guests smile with pleasure over their lunch and watch her bountiful platters empty out in record time. It was immediately gratifying.

Stephanie's Chicken Salad

Serves 2.

(Multiply to feed as many people as you want.)

> 1 large chicken breast, bone-in, skin on
> 2 tablespoons mayonnaise, preferably Hellmann's
> ½ cup slivered almonds, toasted
> 3 tablespoons capers
> Pinch of kosher salt and pinch of white pepper

1. Preheat oven to 375 degrees.
2. Roast chicken breast for 40 minutes or until done. Let cool for an hour.
3. Remove meat from the bone and cut into 1-inch pieces. Mix in the mayonnaise, almonds, and capers.
4. Season with salt and pepper and chill.

As much as I knew about cooking and preparing food, I had no idea how to actually operate a business. I had learned a great deal about business from my time with Steve Wax, but I hadn't yet realized how to apply what I'd learned in the film world to the restaurant business. Besides, Stephi had hired me to cook, not to involve myself in her operations. I had a vague idea that there was a standard P&L equation, a basic 10-15 percent net of total sales, depending on the concept, that a restaurant was supposed to clear in order to be profitable. Through listening to my father and sister discuss the business, I knew that labor should be about 28 to 30 percent of gross sales; food costs varied depending on the concept, but should be roughly 28 to 32 percent of food sales; liquor costs around 18 to 22 percent of liquor sales; and rent should range about 8 to 10 percent of total sales. But I had no clue how the paychecks and food deliveries and all the activity in the kitchen actually translated into those numbers. They held no real weight or meaning. I didn't know how to calculate costs when designing a menu or how to manage a staff where 50 percent of the faces changed from year to year. I didn't know about product mix (PMIX) reports, a crucial tool generated by your point of sale system that analyzes every single food and drink item you sell every day, so you can get an exact picture of what your guests are purchasing, including substitutions and add-ons, and what their choices are costing you. It's key to helping you identify the dogs on your menu, as well as the hits, so you can eliminate waste and control your expenses. For example, you always include a few loss leaders on a menu, like lobster or steak, that typically run at 40 to 50 percent food cost. You also include items like pasta, which is about a 12 percent food cost. Before you open, you can only guess what people are going to like most. If you sell a lot of pasta and very little steak, you're going to make a lot of money. But if it turns out that everyone wants to order the steak and lobster, you could conceivably go out of business if you don't make some adjustments. That's why you've got to monitor your PMIX carefully. It allows you to see problems with your food costs immediately and get control of them before they balloon beyond what your business can support. I learned all of this later through trial by fire in my own restaurants, however, not at Stephi's. Stephanie was a natural. Orderly, methodical, and detail-oriented, she was hands-on and omniscient. But she was still learning. When Stephi had signed her lease back in 1994, much of historic Newbury Street was vacant and she had been able to negotiate an extremely favorable rent. Her business was situated right in the heart of one of Boston's prettiest and most upscale shopping districts, a prime location to attract foot traffic, yet despite its great location, the shop was struggling. The problem definitely wasn't the food, which consistently won raves from the press and from patrons. The problem was that in order to make a food shop really work, you need enormous volume, and Stephi didn't have it. Boston wasn't New York City. Stephi's role models, Eli Zabar and his incomparable E.A.T. on Madison and Eighty-First and Giorgio Deluca's downtown food emporium Dean & Deluca, had both found enormous success with their food shops catering gorgeous food to Manhattanites who would just as soon use their kitchens to store their CD collections as cook. But Boston wasn't New York City. Boston had its wealthy enclaves, but the residents live differently—there are no house charges and people don't order in or take out nearly as often as New Yorkers do. People were not calling up and placing thousand-dollar orders to fill their Cape home refrigerator for the weekend the way Upper East Siders did before heading out to the Hamptons.

Admitting that a concept isn't working has to be the most painful acknowledgment any business owner has to face. But sometimes failure is actually the ticket to success. At this point, you've got two choices. You can throw in the towel and walk away, or you can try a harder tack and stay in the game while rethinking your concept. What you can't do in business is refuse to face reality. Stephi was watching my father learn that lesson the hard way as he tried to keep his own restaurant business afloat, a charming self-serve French fry concept called Pomme Frite, and she wasn't going to repeat his mistakes.

My father's last attempt at restaurant ownership came at the end of a career built through a combination of killer instinct, smart timing, and remarkable business acumen. During the economic boom of the late 1970s and 1980s he made a name for himself as someone who would invest in the kind of small, entrepreneurial businesses big banks would not touch. After Jasper White's incredible rise to culinary fame, Dad became the fairy godfather to every talented chef who dreamed of opening his or her own restaurant, including Charlie Sarkus, Steve DiFillippo, and Todd English. Then the recession of the late 1980s and early 1990s hit, and a lot of real estate loans went south. U.S. Trust, now a $2.2 billion giant, started to wheeze when too many people couldn't repay their real estate loans, and soon bank regulators were scrutinizing the bank and threatening to shut it down unless it could get restored to financial health. In response, in the spring of 1993, the board of directors turned on my father, making him the scapegoat for the bank's troubles and replacing him with a new chief executive. My father had built that bank with his bare hands, and to be pushed out in such a public and humiliating way was an enormous blow.

On top of everything else, he was still recovering from a nearly fatal intestinal embolism that had destroyed 90 percent of his small intestine. My father, who loved to eat more than anything else in the world, woke up from surgery to remove the blood clot to the news that, if he survived, he would be dependent on a chest catheter through which he would receive liquid nutrition. The doctors told him it was unlikely that he would ever eat solid food again.

WHEN I MET FOOD

My father tried to adapt to the catheter and the liquid diet, but a month or so later, after suffering from a severe staph infection entering the catheter, he informed the doctors that he'd rather die than never eat again, and instructed them to take the catheter out and let him try to eat a limited diet of bland, starchy foods like broth, bananas, and yogurt. Miraculously, he not only survived but also over several years expanded his diet to include a wide variety of foods. In fact, because he could only absorb a fraction of the nutrients a man of his age and height normally would, he could eat three times the amount the rest of us did (provided it was fat free) and never gain weight.

Pomme Frite was to be his chance at rebirth, his second career as the entrepreneur he'd always believed himself to be. He had always been enamored with the restaurant world, and he figured that if he could be so successful at spotting talent and helping chefs open restaurants, there was no reason he wouldn't be equally successful in opening his own. In 1993, almost exactly a year after losing his position at the bank, he opened Pomme Frite on a back street in Harvard Square.

The restaurant was a total homage to his beloved Switzerland, with a nod to the fast food automats of his youth. You could order steak and French fries with any kind of topping you wanted on them, including raclette. The fries were hand cut and perfectly crisp, and the steaks were perfectly cooked, so, though the location wasn't ideal, the place did find its followers. But my father wasn't satisfied with opening a restaurant, as he expressed in a 1995 issue of *Restaurant News*: "A single restaurant is a living, but if you want to make money, you have to have a concept and sound expansion to build a sizable company." In accordance with his philosophy, my father decided to expand into our old neighborhood of Chestnut Hill and open a mini version of Pomme Frite—a French fry stand with dipping sauces—in the Burlington Mall.

He had leased two spaces in Chestnut Hill, one that was originally a delicatessen called The Bagel and another that had been the aforementioned Dave Wong's China Sails, where my family used to spend Sunday evenings with our best friends. The Bagel became Pomme Frite. For this location, Dad upgraded the concept a bit and hired staff to wait on guests. But then he made an odd decision. Restaurateurs often like to pay tribute to the restaurant that previously operated in the space they hold, especially if the former restaurant held iconic status. Everyone knew the Bagel, and I guess my father was concerned that its fans would feel like he'd usurped a well-loved neighborhood institution. Or maybe he was just insecure about the solidity of his original concept. The next thing we knew, bagels were showing up on the Pomme Frite menu. And challah. And cheesecake.

When you own a restaurant, you've got to be very clear with the public about who you are. When people decide to go out to eat, they tend to think in terms of food categories: Chinese, Italian, Thai, burgers. Who's going to say, "How about we go to that quasi-Jewish deli Swiss French fry and steak place?" The thing is, people loved the French fries and the steaks. As my father started buying bread ovens and dangerously increasing his overhead, what kept the restaurant going was the quality of the food. But as business dropped off and money started to get tighter, the quality of the food started to suffer, too. Whereas at first Dad was hand cutting his fries, for example, he later switched to frozen ones. This is what happens when owners get reactive instead of proactive—they start to make poor spending decisions that put them into a death spiral. It's natural, because you want to save money.

But as my mother always wisely said, you have to spend money to make money. It is never a sound business decision to compromise on quality to save a few dollars. Every decision you make, from where you buy your meat to whom you select to clean your banquette cushions, is reflected in your guests' experience. The trick is to find a less expensive alternative that actually enhances your food or your space, or at the very least, that will go unnoticed by your guests. If you cheap out on them, they'll notice right away, and they will not come back.

Sadly, that's what happened to Pomme Frite. The confused branding plus the dwindling food quality hurt it beyond salvation, and Dad was forced to close all three restaurants. I learned some big lessons from his experience: be exceedingly clear about your concept and stay true to who you are. Don't let the romance of your dreams get in the way of the business, leading you to buy too much equipment or spend too much on expensive menu items. And if you do invest in your business, don't pass your expenses on to the customer by jacking up the prices. After Pomme Frite, I also became a complete French fry fanatic. Ours are always fresh and hand cut, and woe to the chef on duty if I should come in and spot a pile of limp fries making their way to a table. I should probably share this story with my entire staff—it might help explain my insane fixation on the quality of our fries.

My father was a tenacious guy, determined to move the world in his direction, and his greatest strength and weakness was that he never gave up. My sister is similar in that she does not accept defeat easily, but unlike my father she was rational enough to know that cutting corners to increase profits wasn't the answer and clear-eyed enough to see that her fabulous location and low rent made it advantageous for her to change her dream a little rather than abandon it altogether. After all, people loved her food when they came in to the café to eat; it was the take-out element that was holding her back. Stephanie's instincts told her that if she simply maximized the space where people could enjoy what was by all accounts a lovely atmosphere and delicious food, business would thrive.

Originally, the first thing guests at Stephanie's on Newbury would see upon entering the restaurant was a big glass display case of all the beautiful entrees, salads, and desserts they could order to go. At night, the empty cases resembled forlorn sentinels guarding the kitchen as patrons walked past to get to the dining room. It was a real buzzkill for the dinner business. Once she jettisoned the catering aspect of the business and had no need for the display cases, Stephi had plenty of room to install a chic bar. The impact was meteoric. Almost overnight, Stephi's gross rose from 2.7 million to around 5 million. The bar infused the restaurant with an entirely different vibe, energizing it with the constant hum of action. Dinner business tripled, and even the lunch and brunch crowd grew as hungry shoppers trooped in to rest their feet and gear up for a few more hours in the stores. Since the best way to make money is to fill tables, Stephi also started running promotions to bring people in during the emptiest hours, typically between 4 and 6 p.m. and from 9 to 11 p.m.

Everyone in the family wanted to take credit for the idea to put in the bar—Stephi, my dad, me, and even the GM Stephi hired, Jamie Kaye, who would eventually become my COO—but regardless of who said it first, ultimately it is Stephi who deserves the credit. She was the one who saw the potential in the idea and who made the gutsy move to go forward with it. She didn't have to. She was pregnant with her third child, and selling would have been easy given the desirability of her location. Only she knows how many days and sleepless nights she wrestled with her decision, but in the end she made it alone. It was a bold move, and she was handsomely rewarded for it. It marked the beginning of her establishment not merely as a place to refuel during a shopping trip or the perfect spot for a cozy lunch or brunch, but also as a signature Boston restaurant. I was awestruck by the way she handled this episode in her career.

Stephi would display the same courage three years later, when she tackled yet another, even more dramatic, renovation.

She was smart enough to keep evolving. For years the corner adjacent to her restaurant had been the home of a novelty shop, the kind that sold inappropriate and gaudy greeting cards and tacky bachelorette party accessories. In 2001 they vacated, and the property owner offered Stephi the opportunity to take over their lease. Taking over the corner would give her an additional two thousand square feet of space, but at a price. The landlord was asking a significantly higher amount of money than he had when she first negotiated her lease back in 1994. But Stephi, true to form, knew a good opportunity when she saw it, and decided to make yet another big change. She made the decision to move her bar into the card shop space and add a lounge.

It was an incredibly risky move. She made her decision in the final days of September 2001, just weeks after terrorists had blown America's confidence and sense of security away. The country was reeling, and my parents thought she was crazy to make such an investment, especially at a time when it was possible people would start shying away from crowds and gathering places for fear they could be the next terrorist targets. But Stephi persevered, and she was right. Paradoxically, an interesting phenomenon occurred in urban centers like New York, DC, and Boston after 9/11. In the wake of the attacks, while some people did move out of town and retreat, there was also a resurgence of community spirit. When confronted with tremendous loss, the majority of people seemed to crave contact with their family, friends, and neighbors, and restaurants were packed with people seeking solace in each other's company. It was as though by immersing oneself in the simplest pleasures— a supportive group of friends, a plate of perfect pasta, a bracing glass of good wine—people could reassure themselves and each other that one day things would feel normal again.

Once Stephi claimed the corner and added the lounge, with its deep upholstered chairs and crackling fireplace, Stephanie's on Newbury became one of Boston's premier destinations, where people knew they could consistently experience a sense of belonging and home. People craved comfort food after 9/11, and the odd confluence of 9/11 and Stephi's expansion helped push her brand to the next level.

This is my go-to comfort food.

Mac and Cheese Carbonara

2 cups lumaconi: (or any short shell pasta)
3 tablespoons butter
2 tablespoon flour
1½ cups heavy cream
Pinch of white pepper
Pinch of nutmeg
Pinch of cayenne
3 cups of shredded cheese (Comté, Gruyere, fontina and parmesan)
2 egg yolks
Sea salt

Crust

3 cups Ritz cracker crumbs
¼ cup parmesan cheese
2 pieces crisp bacon
½ cup melted butter

Preheat oven to 350 degrees. Cook lumaconi in boiling salted water according to package directions; drain well and set aside.

Meanwhile, make a béchamel. Melt butter in a medium saucepan over low heat.

Add cayenne, nutmeg, and white pepper.

Blend in flour, stirring constantly, until smooth and bubbly.

Gradually stir in warm cream. Cook, stirring constantly, until mixture boils and thickens, about 10 minutes. Remove from heat.

Take 2 egg yolks and temper them with the béchamel, then fold them into the sauce. This will make the sauce a lot richer. Add 2 cups of the cheese; stir until cheese is melted and sauce is smooth.

Combine sauce with the lumaconi and add salt to taste.

Place in a buttered 2 quart casserole dish.

Spread generously doctored-up Ritz cracker crumbs mixed with ¼ cup Parmesan cheese and chopped crisp bacon, and dot with additional butter and any left over cheese.

Bake 30 to 40 minutes until bubbly and crisp.

———————

By the time Stephanie's on Newbury reopened on the corner, I was no longer working with my sister. But I never forgot what she did for me by offering to let me work in her shop. Stephi gave me solace, a sense of safety, and the chance to get my sanity back after my divorce. And by example, she also gave me three golden rules that would forever stick with me and deeply affect my future decisions as a restaurateur: (1) trust your instincts, (2) claim the corner, and (3) open the door, fall into the bar.

I was inspired and intrigued by the way Stephi successfully navigated risk to build a viable business. Even when I had first wound down my work with Chelsea Pictures and producing, it had been with the thought that when I was ready to ramp up my career again, I would work for myself. I had certainly enjoyed my career in film and I knew that there would still be paths in the film industry, but I had always dreamed about opening my own restaurant, and I thought maybe the time was right. I recognized how hard my sister worked, but I also saw the freedom it granted her to orchestrate her own life. I liked that idea. I would have to manage people of course—chefs, cooks, general managers—but I would be the master of my life and answer to no one but myself. No more studio executives telling me what to do. No more agency creatives, Proctor & Gamble clients, and definitely no more hero balls (which cost a fortune to replace), and no more partners. Except one: Carl.

I met Carl when John and I hired him to renovate the big old beauty of a house we bought in Brookline in 1993. I was looking for a contractor, and very good friends of mine recommended him. The minute I saw him, I liked him. He was forthright, plainspoken, and decent. I was pregnant with my third child and looking forward to fixing up the house for my growing family, and I enjoyed conferring with him as the renovations on the house progressed. He had a daughter the same age as mine that he sometimes brought over. The girls became friends and started to play city basketball together. Carl coached.

Moving into our new home was supposed to mark a happy chapter for my family's future, but instead everything started to go wrong. I lost the baby due to serious complications in my pregnancy. John and I became increasingly distant. We finally split. In the meantime, Carl's own marriage had fallen apart and he had moved into a house in Brookline. During the time that I was working in Stephi's kitchen, we started dating, and a year later we moved in together.

In many ways, Carl and I were complete opposites. Though over the years I have managed to expand his food horizons and refine his taste to the point where he can often be insufferable when we go out to eat, he is at heart a simple, practical guy. His signature dish is a mean tuna fish sandwich, with tons of Hellmann's mayonnaise and tiny minced onions, occasionally topped with bacon and sharp cheddar cheese. Because he is so gentle and self-deprecating, you'd never know how shrewd and tough he really is unless you found yourself opposite him at a negotiating table. He started with nothing and built a multimillion-dollar construction company from the ground up. I have never known anyone with as tireless a work ethic, and he taught me a tremendous amount about business. In return, I have taught him how to live with a little more abandon, to have a little more fun. We may still be opposites, but we complement each other beautifully.

Carl's Tuna Salad

Makes 4 large tuna sandwiches

3 cans of Bumble Bee Solid White tuna packed in water
1 sweet Vidalia onion finely minced
7 tablespoons Hellmann's mayonnaise
Garlic powder
Onion powder
Sea salt
8 slices cheddar cheese
8 strips crisp bacon
Crisp iceberg wedge
Sliced red onion
Thick-sliced ripe tomatoes
4 large Thomas' English muffins

Open tuna cans and squeeze as much water out as possible. Flake the tuna into fine pieces. Don't wash the tuna.

Mix the tuna with finely minced onions and Hellmann's mayonnaise. Add garlic and onion powder and sea salt. Refrigerate until very well chilled.

Cook the bacon until crisp either in the broiler or in a pan. Slice tomatoes and onions about ¼-inch thick. Tear lettuce to top sandwich. Set aside.

Griddle the extra large English muffins.

Top English muffin with tuna fish and coat generously with cheddar cheese and broil until cheese is melted. Add BLT topping. And enjoy.

From the very beginning, when my restaurant dream was nothing but a glimmer of an idea, Carl was my biggest supporter, and I quickly realized that if I wanted to continue to have him in my life, I was going to have to back down from my tendency to go it alone. I wasn't sure how involved I wanted him to be in my work, but he wanted a real partnership, in love and in business, and he would have nothing less. And thank God for that. In the years that we've been together I've come to understand that a successful business is almost always bolstered by strong partnerships, either personal or professional. A partnership that is both personal and professional, however, gives your business a significant advantage. It's exceedingly challenging to run a business and a life together, of course. The restaurant grapevine is filled with stories of chef and spouse partnerships that split after one of the pair finds the other in the walk-in with another member of the staff. But the business can also be like a child you give birth to and nurture together, reinforcing your connection to each other and keeping you intimately involved in the other's life.

I trust Carl like I've never trusted anyone. His work in construction prepared him perfectly for the nickel and dime restaurant world. He is my second set of eyes, running the financial side of the business, crunching all the numbers, scanning the fine print on every document. We clash—I tend to see big, he tends to see what big really costs. I go with my intuition, he's extremely detail oriented and structured. He is involved in all the real estate deals, he builds the restaurants, he analyzes the operations, and I'm the big picture person. I am grateful that he pushes back so much, because it allows me the freedom to think creatively, knowing that he is there behind me to make sure that my pie-in-the-sky ideas are workable. Together, we end up making smarter, stronger decisions than we would alone. He is the biggest gift in my life, and any success I've achieved in the years since I left Stephi's shop has been sweeter because he was a part of it.

Six

Claiming the Corner

I felt like the dots of my life were connecting in a way that was too powerful to ignore. I had always loved being around and talking about food, and building a restaurant business just made sense. The more I thought about it, the more excited I got. My best friend, Jayne, thought I was crazy. In the most cautious, loving way possible, she sat me down and urged me to reconsider. It was too hard, she said. The risks were too high. I could be ruined. Her warning carried a great deal of weight because Jayne was a new business owner herself. A year earlier she and her business partner had opened a cosmetics store in Greenwich, Connecticut, called The Beauty Bar. The motto was "Beauty. Body. Brains." It was a gorgeous shop, and her graphics and concept were brilliant. Yet Jayne and her partner had a difference of opinion about what the business was supposed to be. Jayne wanted to brand it as a high-end cosmetics store like Sephora and her partner thought it should be more of a high-end mani/pedi salon. As a result of confusing branding messages, the business was struggling. They were forced to put more money in and, as expected, that is when things started to fall apart.

I spent several weeks mulling her words over carefully, but

I finally came to the conclusion that, though Jayne might be right and I might be crazy, I still had to try. I couldn't see any other path to follow. Starting my own business was the only way I could ensure that, whatever happened, I would be master of my own destiny,

Jayne, it should be noted, transcended her difficult experience in the beauty business and used the lessons she learned to turn herself into a brand with a website and radio show called "A Fashionable Life." Now she is sought out as a fashion expert by ABC, CNBC, WWD, and Martha Stewart, bolstering my theory that no matter where life takes us, it's always closer to where we are supposed to be. Thanks to Jayne, I also met Chris Tinnesz, the extraordinarily talented man who had done the graphics for the Beauty Bar. Chris had worked for Ralph Lauren and Tommy Hilfiger, and he did the Pink campaign for Victoria's Secret. I am insanely picky and hands-on with my logos and graphics. Nothing is more important than perfecting the subliminal message you want the public to absorb about your restaurant even before they drive up to your door. For eight years Chris has branded all my restaurants. I can give him one word and he can create endless, wildly different visual interpretations of it, each one more creative and illuminating than the next. I consider him one of the most professional creative geniuses I have ever met.

I didn't crystallize my business idea right away. For about three years, from 1999 to 2003, I focused almost exclusively on my kids. I accepted some freelance film production work, but for the most part, I relished all the stay-at-home mom activities that I had missed out on during the early years of my career. Whereas once I was jetting off to exotic locales at a moment's notice, now I was schlepping back and forth in the Land Cruiser, making lunches, and running the penny candy station for the annual school fair. John had always been around for the kids when I was traveling or working long hours, but now that he was gone, it was up to me to provide an extra sense of stability. On one hand, I was lucky that I had decided to take a step back from my career before the dissolution of my marriage, so that the divorce didn't force me into it. On the other hand, even with the money I brought home from working in Stephi's shop I feared that I wouldn't be able to continue to provide for the kids what had been possible with our dual salaries.

Fortunately, the real estate bubble solved that problem. In 2000 I sold my house for an excellent price and none of us wanted for anything between the money left over from the sale and the income I brought in with the freelance work I started taking on here and there, when it didn't conflict with my kids' schedules. Somewhere along the way, however, I started carrying a little notebook around with me. In it, I started jotting menu and design ideas for a restaurant I had yet to name.

I was not the only one in the family in a state of reinvention. Although he had long ago remarried, my father was no longer the debonair Captain Jack. His life had taken a hard turn. Almost by sheer force of will alone, he had defeated his doctors' pessimistic predictions and had made a slow but steady recovery from the aftereffects of his intestinal embolism. At the same time, he was struggling against a severe heart condition that had robbed him of much of the energy he needed to live the active lifestyle of sailing and skiing that he loved. But he would not give up. He got on the treadmill, he figured out how to eat as well as his battered body would allow him, and he powered on. Yet understandably, between his health crises and his professional setbacks, it took him a while to regain his confidence.

He didn't need to look far to see reminders of his accomplishments and business acumen. By now Jack Sidell's influence on the Boston restaurant scene had become mythic, transforming the city from a reliable purveyor of lobster and baked beans to a spectacular culinary destination. Jasper White, Lydia Shire,

Barbara Lynch, Gordon Hamersley, Steve DiFillippo, Charlie Sarkus—all had gone on to become modern-day celebrity chefs and restaurateurs, and all of them had my father to thank for giving them the initial loans that permitted them to open their first restaurants. One chef, Todd English, had opened one of his famous Figs locations in the former Pomme Frite space in Chestnut Hill, sandwiched between Dave Wong's China Sails and a travel agency on the corner. He had bought the business from my father with a cash down payment, and was making monthly payments for the remaining amount due.

In 2003 I started looking in earnest for a space where I could open a restaurant. I was in a fortunate position—I didn't need to raise outside money and was beholden to no one because I was able to finance the project through my own capital and contributions from my family. Then my father came to me with a proposal. Would I consider taking over the space currently occupied by Figs? Todd English's investors were pressuring him to sell because they weren't comfortable with him sharing some of the facilities with his other restaurant, Olives, which was owned by a separate set of investors. I could buy the space from Todd and take over his debt to my father. I wasn't excited by the idea. The strip mall location was uninspiring, and Chestnut Hill was not what I had been thinking when I told myself I was ready to make my mark on the Boston dining landscape. But my father wouldn't listen. He seemed especially eager that his younger daughter get a shot at the restaurant biz, and that he be the person to give it to her. Maybe he knew his time was limited, and he saw this as his last chance to get closer to me. Maybe he liked the idea of having both of his daughters be a part of his legacy in shaping the Boston restaurant scene. Maybe he knew he didn't have the stamina anymore to open his own restaurant and he wanted to live vicariously through me. Regardless, it clearly meant so much to him that saying no almost didn't feel like an option. And I confess it felt good to be sought out after pursuing him so long for attention.

The next thing I knew I was talking to Todd about buying his equipment, and my father had set up meetings for me with the manager of Todd's company and with the landlord for the Chestnut Hill location. As we negotiated, there was one detail about which I was adamant: I had to have the corner. The broker would lease me the space currently held by the travel agency, or we had no deal. I've always had this thing about the corner, and watching how Stephi's business boomed as soon as she took over the corner on her block only reinforced my preference. The corner, inside and outside a restaurant, is a power location. From outside, you're noticeable from three angles. You've got a little more to work with, the option of designing for a little more drama and curb appeal. If you watch an empty dining room fill up, the corners get occupied first. On the inside, the corner is the premier seat, the best place from which to see and to be seen. It gives you greater control—your back and sides are protected but you also have the best vantage point from which to survey a room. Neither Todd nor my dad took the corner, and I'm sure they didn't give it much thought, but I insisted. If I was going to open in suburban Massachusetts and the land of strip malls, I wanted to punctuate the banal landscape with a landmark exterior design.

And so I took over Todd English's debt to my father, and the lease was mine. I'll never agree to a deal that doesn't allow me to transfer my lease. No restaurateur ever should. Ideally, you should own your own real estate, but that's an expensive proposition. Until you can afford to be your own landlord, make sure you have control over your lease. It's a powerful asset.

Chestnut Hill wasn't necessarily the location I would have chosen for my first restaurant, but you can't turn your nose up at opportunity just because it doesn't fit the ideal you had in mind. When the door of opportunity opens, you need to be damn well ready to spot it and walk through. I could see this was one of those times, and that made my decision easier.

When I was in my thirties I had noticed that many of the women around me were often paralyzed by indecision. I worked with female directors on commercials who couldn't decide the color of their own socks, much less whether we needed another take. Maybe that fear of decision making explains why there were so few female directors in the first place—the job is all about making quick decisions. Come to think of it, maybe that explains why male owners, too, dominate the restaurant world. Women, far more than men, are afraid to be wrong. I overcame that tendency early on by realizing that indecision only leads to confusion, which almost guarantees failure. I decided it was better to be wrong and move on than to be indecisive. At least when you're wrong you'll get somewhere new—maybe not where you originally hoped to be, but somewhere. Indecisiveness just leaves you stuck.

I've been asked several times whether it has been difficult to be a woman in the male-dominated restaurant world. It hasn't. My dad was tough on me, but he did instill in me the belief that anything was possible if I was willing to work for it. The Brunching with Barclay series was a marketing tactic, but it also stemmed from his support for women's equality. He liked the idea of bringing women into a man's world and doing his part to help inspire them. My best friends have always been men, I'm comfortable with men, and by the time I got into the restaurant business I had plenty of real-world experience. I entered the business world believing I was on a level playing field. I knew how to command respect, and no one was going to mess with me. As a young woman in the film industry, I saw how the attention from older men could be lethal to your career if you allowed it to divert your ambition or compromise your values. To survive, you had be smart and clear about your objective and not let anyone woo you away from your goals with pretty promises and flattery. That said, knowing how to manage one's sexuality correctly can be a huge asset—there is a great advantage to knowing how to walk the razor thin line between harmless and harmful flirting.

I didn't worry about being beholden to my dad. He was tired, and I could tell that this project would give him purpose and I was happy to be a part of that. I suspected he would be a pain to deal with sometimes, and I was right—the man could be frustratingly inflexible and stubborn. But the flip side is that he taught me everything he knew, and shared every story about his triumphs and his failures so that I could learn from his example and his mistakes. The information he passed along wasn't exclusively applicable for restaurants—he was passing down his entire business philosophy. After so many years of seeming disinterested, he became my champion. Finally, he was seeing me.

I signed on a couple of dozen dotted lines, and the deal was done. I couldn't keep calling my new project "the restaurant," though. I needed a name. By now the pages of my notebook were filled with names I thought might suit the concept that was starting to develop in my head. But the name "Metropolitan" was always at the top of my list. I liked the comprehensiveness of the word. Something that was metropolitan was worldly, sophisticated, hip, modern, urban, and capable of changing, evolving, and growing. It had movement. The word encompassed city and suburb, and implied culture and sophistication yet also inclusiveness, a willingness to be open to unusual and maybe even surprising combinations. Boston is a conservative food town—the mainstream is only going to go a little way out on a limb with you. With the word "Metropolitan," I could work with a broad, modern international concept within a steak house format; I added the word "Club" because I had been to a Metropolitan Club in New York City that was an elegant and beautiful private club, and I thought invoking that kind of refinement and exclusivity would be particularly appealing to the wealthy residents of Chestnut Hill. It was simply another way to subliminally imply that your restaurant experience would be at once adventurous yet classy and comfortable.

It's interesting to look back at that notebook and see how my ideas for Metropolitan Club developed and changed, but right from the beginning, there were a few things about which I was certain:

1. I wanted to open a blockbuster hit that would launch a string of other hits. I had an excellent model—a popular steak house called Capital Grille that I frequently enjoyed, located about a mile up the road from Figs. Ned Grace, CEO of RARE Hospitality, Inc., had opened the first Capital Grille in Providence, Rhode Island, in 1989. Despite the fact that the country was teetering on the edge of recession, people flocked to book their special occasions and business dinners there. By 1997, four more Capital Grilles had opened up around the country, including the one in Chestnut Hill.

Grace's high-end yet casual concept struck me as the restaurant equivalent to an action film—entertainment that appeals to a wide American audience. I was going to try to capture as many people as possible. I'd be multigenerational, a perfect setting for a Mother's Day brunch, a romantic first date, or a business dinner. I'd be the place where everyone at the table could easily find something they wanted to eat. Too many times I'd gone out to dinner with my family and at least one of us would feel like we had to compromise. I'd want a salad, Carl would want a steak, Ali would clamor for pasta, and Ben would have to have a burger. Even Capital Grille didn't serve all of that. If I could brand myself as truly "metropolitan"—that is, offering something special for everyone—I would give myself total flexibility as I conceived of the subsequent restaurants that would grow my business.

MET Signature Steak Sauce

Makes 3 to 4 cups

    5 ounces capers
    5 ounces garlic
    5 ounces anchovies
    1 ½ pounds bacon
    2 pounds Spanish onions
    1 cup golden raisins
    1 ½ cups brown sugar
    1 cup molasses
    1 cup red wine vinegar
    ½ can of tomato paste
    1 ½ can of tomato filet
    5 ounces jalapeno, minced
    1 ½ cups Worcestershire sauce
    2 heaping tablespoons Dijon mustard
    2 tablespoons butter

In food processor, puree capers, garlic, and anchovies. In large nonreactive pan caramelize the capers, garlic, and anchovy mix. Add bacon and render until golden brown. Add onions and caramelize. Add golden raisins and brown sugar. When sugar melts, add molasses and the red wine vinegar. Allow the vinegar to reduce by half. Add tomato paste. Continue to cook. Add tomato filet, jalapenos, and Worcestershire. Cook for 1 ½ hours until flavors have melded. Finish with butter and mustard while mixing. Cool and refrigerate.

Only later, when I was figuring out the name of my second restaurant, would I realize that I had given myself a goldmine of a branding opportunity. After all, how many times do we meet others for a meal, a snack, or a drink? And when we think back upon those encounters, what do we say? We met for lunch. We met for coffee, for dinner, or for cocktails. A place that is "metropolitan" is a place that is big enough for everyone, where people from all walks of life can come to connect with others and find their place in the world. Ultimately, I wanted "Met" to become code for, "that place where you can be yourself and have a great time." If I could pull that off, the actual name of the restaurant wouldn't matter anymore. The word "Met" would tell people what they needed to know.

2. I wanted to go big. There would be none of those teensy servings that were becoming de rigueur at high-end establishments; the food was going to cover the plate. There wasn't anything especially groundbreaking about going big. But rarely had anyone seen such hearty portions of the quality that I intended to provide. The high quality would make the difference.

3. My restaurant would be meat centric but there would be fabulous options for women interested in eating something lighter, too. And my offerings wouldn't feel like begrudging afterthoughts or boring diet food, either, like the ubiquitous side salad, Caesar salad, or iceberg wedge that you could find on just about every steak house menu in the country. If we

were going to serve salads, they would be amazing, exciting salads that people would talk about as much as our steaks: a Chinatown salad that was an interpretation of a duck salad I had at Le Caprice in London, with crispy duck morsels, carrots, cucumber, and plum sauce, combined with Susur Lee's mountain of beautiful slaw of julienned Chinese vegetables; or what I called the Monday salad, which I made for my kids—because who wants to cook on Monday?—with butter lettuce topped with Marcona almonds, pulled chicken, bacon, avocado, and Comté; or a combination of my favorite Los Angeles chopped salads from the Polo Lounge, La Scala, and the Ivy. Ours would have a combination of micro-chopped iceberg and romaine—one for crunch, one for texture—eight-minute just-hard-cooked eggs, sweet roasted red beets, raw broccoli, double-smoked bacon lardons, tangy shredded cheddar cheese, creamy ripe avocado, almost-undetectable red onions, and just about everything else you can imagine (that salad became one of our most popular signature dishes). The Paris-inspired duo of tuna and salmon tartare, the trio of beets, the salmon burger, carpaccio three ways—all were dishes developed for women who wanted to eat well and not hate themselves in the morning.

My motivation was partly just good business. I knew that if I could provide options packed with flavor but not too many calories, women would come to me and bring their dates and their families as well. Women are the decision makers in the household when it comes to where to dine out. But I was also mostly motivated by a sense of sisterhood. If I could change anything in this world it would be the fact that food can make you fat. Since I can't, I do my best to put items on the menu that women can enjoy without feeling guilty. I want to be thin, but I sure as hell don't want to go through life not eating, and I don't think other women should, either.

Original Metropolitan Club Caesar Dressing

Makes 3 cups

> Heaping tablespoon of Dijon mustard
> 2 egg yolks
> 1 whole egg
> 2 garlic cloves slivered
> 2 anchovy filets
> 2 to 3 cups avocado oil
> ½ cup Parmigiano Reggiano
> Juice of whole lemon
> Heavy dash Worcestershire sauce
> ¼ to ½ cup muscat vinegar
> Salt
> Cayenne
> Cracked black pepper

Put garlic cloves and anchovy in a wooden bowl. Mash with a fork to season the bowl. Add mustard and eggs and combine with a whisk. Slowly pour the oil into mustard/egg/garlic/anchovy mixture in a steady stream and incorporate until emulsified. It looks close to a mayonnaise. Add juice of lemon, muscat vinegar, and Worcestershire. Add cheese, pepper, and cayenne. Season to taste.

---

4. My restaurant would be known as a place where people would always get what they wanted. For example, I had noticed that people were starting to eat dinner at the Capital Grille bar, going so far as to call ahead to reserve seats there. To me that signified a shift, that people were starting to crave a more casual and social environment when they ate out. They

couldn't get that very often at Capital Grille, however, because the bar could only seat about fourteen to twenty people, and it often filled up. In fact, there really wasn't anywhere in Chestnut Hill that people could eat an elegant meal in a casual bar atmosphere. But if that's what people wanted, that's what I would provide. Here was the opportunity to define my niche. I decided to create a fabulous bar lounge, one that could be a destination in and of itself.

I also developed a separate bar menu. This was something that just hadn't been done before in better restaurants. None of the models for my restaurants—the Palms and the Mortons and the Capital Grilles of the world—had bar menus in addition to the regular menu. Instead of peanuts, I'd serve truffled popcorn. Instead of a menu dominated by dishes of melted or fried cheese in various forms, you could get crunchy duck spring rolls. And if you were really craving a bar staple, our wings and calamari would be the best you'd ever had. Like the selections on our regular dinner and lunch menus, everything would look and taste decadent, but the experience would be decidedly casual. It was, luckily enough, exactly what people wanted. Almost years later, you still can't get into the bar on Saturday nights.

_____

MET Bar Chicken Wings with Special Salt

Serves 8 to 10

> 4 pounds extra large chicken wings, brine overnight in the refrigerator
>
> 3 quarts of water
>
> 1 cup sugar
>
> 1 cup kosher salt
>
> Handful of black peppercorns
>
> 4 bay leaves

Remove from brine and dry. Preheat oven and roast for onr hour.

Remove from oven. You can refrigerate at this point and finish later or put directly on the grill. Cook on the grill until you get a nice char—flipping accordingly. Once you remove from the grill, toss chicken in the special salt below.

Special Salt Rub:
Combine:
- ¼ cup brown sugar
- ¼ cup onion powder
- ¼ cup garlic powder
- ¼ cup paprika
- ⅛ cup honey powder
- ⅛ cup jalapeno powder
- ⅛ cup cayenne powder
- 1 ½ tablespoons kosher salt
- Pinch of thyme

Once the chicken is tossed with salt, finish under broiler until crisp. Serve with honey mustard.

———————————

One more thing. Diners who chose to eat in the dining room would be allowed, even encouraged, to order off the bar menu. The Everything Girl in me couldn't imagine a better setup—one location, two dining alternatives to suit any mood. My servers, it turned out, would not be so thrilled. Early on I had battles with my waitstaff in the dining room because I instructed them to give a bar menu and a restaurant menu to every guest. They balked, believing that it would lower their average ticket price. My answer to that was, suggest a cocktail or a bottle of wine, and don't let the guest walk away without dessert. The waiters weren't wrong—in the short term the average ticket would be lower when people were ordering burgers instead of rib eyes. Conversely, however, the sales volume went way, way up.

When people know they can get what they want, they come back again and again. I have to train my waiters to think beyond one meal and one experience—if these guests can get a hamburger one night and a steak the next they might come in two times a week instead of one, thereby filling the restaurant's coffers and the waiters' pockets. This long-term concept is vital to our business and yet extremely hard to impart to people who live paycheck to paycheck. When waiters leave their jobs to go open the next busy restaurant, they often say they are following the money. What they don't realize is that it is in their power to create a place where the money always is if they give the guests what they want. Finding staff who are mature enough and committed enough to take this long view is a challenge in any business, but especially in an industry whose workers so often consider their jobs a temporary stop on the way to something else. It's not like the film industry, where people are so hungry to break in they will do anything to get a job. That's why, when I spot someone who really seems made for the restaurant business, I will go all out to nurture his talent and give him opportunities to see that restaurant work does not have to be just a job, but can also be a fulfilling and exciting career.

5. I wanted to give people a sense of "Wow!" When I was a little girl my parents would take me to the Four Seasons, and at the end of the meal the waiter would bring out a big vat of cotton candy. It was a total delight, and that's why I serve cotton candy whenever I can, whether it's to small children for dessert or as a fun element in a cocktail. It's not easy to do—cotton candy machines are big and bulky and expensive to maintain, but the reaction when people see the cotton

candy come out in all its spun-sugar glory, the big smiles and the wide, sparkling eyes? Priceless.

At the time I was conceiving of MET Club I hadn't thought of the cotton candy yet, but I knew I could delight people with beautiful flavors, generous portions, creativity, originality, and stellar service. Yet I wanted people to know they were in for something special even before they walked through the door. It is said that you have about five seconds to make a first impression when guests walk into your restaurant, but in reality their impression is set before they set foot across your threshold. The very door handle your guest has to grasp to walk into your establishment should convey some kind of message, and at the very least should feel appealing and inviting in his grip. I wanted people to start anticipating a great evening even before they got out of their cars. I had a challenge on my hands with the very location of my restaurant.

American suburbia is the land of strip malls, and Chestnut Hill, despite being an especially pretty suburb, was no different from any other in that regard. Our shopping centers are tasteful, but they're strips nonetheless, which explains why suburban businesses' curb appeal is often limited. That's why I insisted on claiming the coveted corner where the travel agency was once located—it gave me options. I wanted to find a way to punctuate the landscape and announce to anyone passing by that at Metropolitan Club they would find something different and exciting. Carl and I pushed the corner about six feet further out from the rest of the strip to create a rotunda-style entryway lined with floor-to-ceiling windows all the way around. From the outside, it created a graceful, inviting curve that caught the eye of any passersby who had become completely sedated by the row after row of predictably flat business facades lining the road. From the inside, the unusual shape of the vestibule made people feel like they were making a grand entrance. From the vestibule they could be led straight into our large bar lounge or ushered into the main dining area.

I extended the high-end feel throughout the restaurant. The seats were covered in warm saddle leather; recessed lighting, wall sconces, and a red back-painted glass fireplace all gave the interior a rich glow. We created oversized menus with beautiful copper covers. MET Club felt like the sophisticated New York City steak house BLT Steak: modern, cushy, and costly, the kind of place you go to celebrate special occasions. It was an expensive decision. Carl and I thought it would cost about $1.5 million to open the restaurant, and in the end it cost about $2 million. It looked beautiful, but maybe I shouldn't have insisted on the perfect furnishings and high quality smallwares, like exquisite china, Laquille steak knives, and copper pots for serving pot pie, especially when we found that within months plates were shattered, knives were stolen, and the plateware didn't matter as much as what was served on it. Aesthetic details such as these can drive business, and being known for a few signature flourishes goes a long way, but splurging on items that have to be continuously replaced at high cost is irresponsible.

I made one decision that proved to be more fateful than I ever could have anticipated. There were no visible bars in the neighborhood and I wanted people to know one had finally arrived, so I put a huge copper sign outside announcing the MET Bar, which we lit up at night. We called the bar the MET Bar inside the MET Club, and we placed a big letter "M" like a sentinel on top of the rotunda. We were motivated by the power of minimalist design but also by the fact that "Metropolitan" was too long to fit. In the end, the name "Metropolitan Club" only appears etched in small letters on the glass of the front doors. It's no wonder the entire location, restaurant and bar, became known as the MET Bar. I loved the idea of providing a venue within a venue, but I had no idea that the dual identity I developed would create some difficult branding issues. For example, it used to be problematic when people called 411 to get our phone number and didn't realize that MET Bar wasn't our real name. That's an easy fix. Now we're listed as MET Bar, MET Club, and Metropolitan Club. But MET is definitely our core brand, and I market the business accordingly. As time has passed, we seem to have resolved any confusion about who we are.

6.   The surprise would be that, despite its luxuriousness, Metropolitan Club would offer value. I never lose sight of how hard it is to make a buck. That was one of the reasons I developed a bar menu: people would discover that they could have a fantastic, filling meal for less than $20, and still feel like they had just treated themselves to something special. If I executed my vision correctly, however, I was sure people would feel they'd gotten a good value even after ordering the expensive items on my menu. A $54 Allen Brothers prime sirloin steak is expensive, no doubt about it. But what if it's the best steak you've ever eaten? What if you're still thinking about that steak three days later, regretting the few pieces you couldn't finish? That's the experience I was going for. But you don't achieve that merely by delivering a product commensurate with the price; you achieve it by exceeding expectations.

MET Fries with Truffle Mayo

Makes 4 large portions

6 large Idaho potatos or Yukon Golds
2 quarts canola or peanut oil

Cut potatoes, leaving skin on into ¼-inch-wide fries. Rinse to get rid of any excess starch or sugar. Store in water with lemon juice (1 tablespoon to one gallon of water ratio). This will prevent them from turning black. Drain the water, dry the fries, and deep fry until limp. Do not cook through. Cool and refrigerate. Cover well. Fry at 350 degrees, no higher, until crisp and golden brown. Serve with dipping sauce below.

Combine:
    2 cup Hellmann's mayonnaise
    ⅛ cup truffle oil
    ½ cup grated parmesan cheese
    ¼ cup white vinegar
    Sea salt to taste

————————

When I first opened, my managers and I spent hours debating the size of our pours and the feel of the glasses in which our drinks would be served. A place is judged by the size of its drinks. The average mixed drink contains one-and-a-half to two ounces of alcohol, and most restaurants serve four- to five-ounce glasses of wine. We put three to four ounces in every mixed drink, and guests enjoy their wine in seven- to eight-ounce glasses. The cost of our drinks are commensurate with most places, but it's rare that people don't smile when they see their big, solid drinks arrive (much like they do when they get their first glimpse of a poof of cotton candy.

They're a lot happier than they would have been elsewhere when their drink arrived in a tiny glass and they wondered what exactly they were paying for. It's not the amount of money you spend on something that gives it value, it's the amount you enjoy it. I wanted people to experience the same generosity they would receive if I were having them to dinner in my home. I knew that people would not begrudge spending money at my restaurant as long as I could consistently meet and even exceed their expectations. I quickly discovered that perception matters a great deal, however, and I was reminded that despite my best efforts, I really wouldn't be able to please everyone. Even though our pours are bigger than average, so are our glasses, which means that they aren't filled all the way to the top. To some people, that's all that matters. The first week we were open a customer smashed his glass on the bar and growled irritably, "Fill. My. Glass. To. The. Top!" I considered switching to smaller glasses, but I couldn't. A small glass just wouldn't give my guests that sense of "Wow" when their drink arrived, and I thought that feeling would drive the business more than capitulating to a few individuals looking for a reason to complain.

My notebook outlined everything I wanted to accomplish with this restaurant. Now I needed a team to help me bring all of my ideas to life. I had had such a great experience working with my two best friends, Hank and Bob, creating magic in commercials and movies. I knew it would be hard to reproduce that kind of cerebral and emotional connection that the three of us had, but I hoped to try. At the very least, I knew I needed to be a good judge of character if I was going to grow a business like the kind I had in mind, because I knew that eventually I wouldn't be able to be on site all the time. I didn't want an experience like that of my friend Marty Bloom, who owned a chain of restaurants called Vinny Testa's. Over time, he noticed that his food costs were rising at one of his Philadelphia locations, and he asked his general manager whether someone could be stealing. The general manager said he'd look into it. In the meantime, Marty booked a flight to Philly with a pair of night-vision goggles packed in his bag. He planted himself on a lawn chair across the street from his restaurant and, camouflaged by the dark, watched as people came in and out of the back door all night, loading steaks into a cooler next to the trash bin. In the end, he was forced to change his whole management team.

I would only be as strong as the team I pulled together. I needed to find people I could trust, but also people who could see my vision and communicate it to others. I also needed to find people who would complement my own strengths and weaknesses.

Aside from the owner, the general manager is the heart and soul of a restaurant, as much, if not more so, than the chef. A great GM drives the business, so that's where I began. After all, the restaurant can survive if the chef is antisocial as long as she excels at cooking, food planning, prep, budgeting, and hiring a solid team for the back of the house, including sous chefs, dishwashers, prep cooks, and the receiver who evaluates the products we buy to make sure we're not being short-changed by vendors. The general manager, however, needs to be a kind of Renaissance man (or woman). He is the equivalent of a producer on a film, responsible for making sure that everything that happens within the four walls of the restaurant leads to a great experience for the guests. It's a huge job. He hires, fires, trains, and schedules the whole team that works the front of the house, such as the assistant managers, the hosts, the waitstaff, and support staff. He is also in charge of budgeting, ordering supplies (including toilet paper) and managing guest relations.

Once again, I turned to Capital Grille for inspiration. Their GM, Richard, was extraordinary, a real old-school maitre d'. One of the main reasons Capital Grille was such a wonderful place to be was because it had Richard at the helm, keeping an eye on all the behind-the-scenes aspects of the business, while making everyone who walked through the door feel like he'd just been welcomed into Richard's home. When Richard greeted you, you almost believed that he had been waiting all night just to see your face.

Capital Grille could allow its managers to be out on the floor all the time because the corporation took care of the mountains of paperwork it takes to keep a business running smoothly. That wasn't an option for us, so I wanted to hire someone who was equal parts entertainer, businessman, politician, and counselor, and I found those ideal characteristics in Mark Peterson. I had met Mark when he worked for Richard at Capital Grille. He was a manager, not a general manager, and he left Cap Grille to go and work for a big, very popular bar called City Bar. Yet from the minute I met him I was certain that he was the guy I needed. I've said that chemistry is extremely important in business relationships, and Mark and I had it. Plus, he was a control freak who would lose sleep over the smallest details. I liked that. Like Carl, he'd sweat the small stuff so I could be free to grow the business. As a bonus, Mark already had a team in mind that he wanted to bring on board: Steve Zeneski, a charismatic, attractive, generous but responsible operator with the gift of gab and the ability to handle his guests flawlessly, and Beau Sturm, who was a rock star bartender and manager. My bases would be covered—a dining room manager, a bar manager, and an overall GM who had great classic old-school restaurant training with strong organizational and operation skills.

As I look back, the people who helped me launch MET Club were an amazing group who helped make that chapter in the restaurant's history special. It's almost a shame we came together so early, because it would be hard to duplicate that level of teamwork and sense of connection. I always tell my team now that hiring great talent and great passion is our utmost priority. You're only as good as your weakest link, whether in the office or on the line. Talent can come in surprising forms, and training goes a long way in bringing out the best in people, but to be successful you must also look for people who are passionate about what they do, whether it's washing a dish, or creating a dish. Without that passion on your side, you won't get far. I learned this when I was a film producer. I excelled at analyzing a commercial in paper form, when it was just a bit of dialogue and images, and breaking it down into dollars—How many locations could we hit in a day? How much equipment would we need?—so that we could calculate how much it would cost to shoot. I had to figure out how to put a high quality product out for as little money as possible, because budgets were tight. And I discovered that achieving this was only possible when you could attract talent who liked the project so much they were willing to do whatever it took to make it come to life. The same thing goes for restaurants. Your team has to be passionate, because you all have to feel that you're invested in the project— in this case, the restaurant—together. Your waitstaff's passion for the food they're serving to their guests should be infectious. Your chef has to be passionate if he's going to successfully build relationships and negotiate with vendors to get the best quality product for a fair price. Your management team should be as passionate about growing the business as you are.

Even with the great team I had in place, however, I faced a steep learning curve. I still didn't know much about payments, receivables, taxes, and payrolls—all the details specific to running a restaurant business. I figured if I trusted these three guys enough to hire them, all with more experience in the industry than I, all I could do was try to listen hard to what they said.

Next, I needed someone to help me execute the menu ideas that I had been feverishly jotting down in my notebook. Lydia Shire had hired a talented and creative chef named Jeff Fournier for her restaurant Locke-Ober, Boston's third-oldest restaurant, and later for her luxury steak house, Excelsior. A painter, Jeff was known for unusual and eclectic combinations and fun, artistic presentations that I thought would fit in perfectly with what I envisioned for MET Club. I hoped he would consider my restaurant a platform opportunity. He did, and he proceeded to create a lovely menu.

Jeff excelled at making food that was as beautiful to look at as it was to eat. He would cream purple potatoes or sweet potatoes and punctuate the plate, drawing long strips of bright orange or dotting it with purple. My parents were very supportive of MET Club but they couldn't stand Jeff's presentation. I didn't care. I thought it was fantastic and delightfully "Wow."

Just a few months before MET Club opened, my father moved in with Carl, Ben, and me (Ali was now studying at Brown University). Though my dad owned an apartment on the waterfront, he had rented it some years earlier and he needed a place to stay for a short while. His second marriage had ended, and I was sympathetic to his pain. It was an unusual time for us. He was respectful of our space and demanded very little, and in these short months he and I, and he and my son, got the chance to know each other in a daily way that we had not been afforded since my high school years. He was a tremendous support as I made my way through the last throes of building the restaurant.

The team and I worked like crazy people until the very last second, and then it was show time. On November 24, 2004, we opened our doors to a select group of family and friends. Despite the friendly crowd, I was anxious. It was a familiar sensation. I'd had it while sitting in darkened movie theatres anticipating the exact moment before the show starts. Then, as my staff and I greeted the parade of people spilling in, I was flooded with remarkable calm, and I felt at that moment that this was what I was built for—this was what I was meant to do.

As the evening wore on I chatted with our guests, many of whom I knew very well, to gauge their reaction. What did they think? Was I delivering what they wanted? Was this a place they could make their own? Would they come back once or twice a week? These were questions that would plague me and that I couldn't possibly answer for many years to come, but I was eager to fast-forward to find out if we were going to be okay, if we were going to survive.

You never know how the public is going to receive what you create and put out into the world, whether it's a new restaurant, a menu item, a piece of art, or a film. That's why you have to be made of some pretty strong stuff to go into creative fields—otherwise the potential for rejection is so high the stress will kill you. You can hedge your bets by doing the research and staying current and taking smart creative and financial risks, but the truth is that only the test of time will tell you whether you have a lasting success on your hands. Even if you see immediate success, there is no way to know whether the magic you've created—the magic all of us in creative businesses aim to create—is fleeting and ephemeral or long lasting and memorable.

All I wanted, as my guests arrived from the chilly night air into my warm, elegant lobby, was that they would get what I was trying to create, and that they would like it. My head was filled with questions and doubts. Why did I think I could pull this off any better than my father, or with anything close to my sister's skill? What was I thinking, opening a restaurant not just in my hometown, but in the neighborhood where I grew up, where the criticism would surely be more pointed—Jack Sidell's daughter! Stephanie Sidell's sister!—and there would be nowhere to hide if I failed?

Over time, I figured out that if I'm afraid to do something, it's probably because it's worth doing, and so, as Stephen Mindich advised me years before, I learned not to see fear as my enemy but as my ally. The hardest fear to overcome since I started in this business has been the fear of rejection, the fear that not everyone will love me. That has been a hard lesson for me to accept. Maybe it's a hard lesson for many women to accept. But if you're going to stay in this business, you have no choice. I'm fifty-five now, and finally, I can say that I care a lot less what people think. It's liberating.

Almost eight years ago, though, on the opening night of my first restaurant, I was still afraid. And yet I realized that, regardless of what the future brought, I had taken a major leap, and for that alone I was proud. I wasn't sure if I would wind up where I had planned, but at least I wasn't going to be stuck. One way or another, I was going to be just fine.

Seven

Bathroom Stalls Are for Sex, and Other Things I Learned

From the minute Metropolitan Club officially opened to the public, we were packed. People spoke with enthusiasm about how much the restaurant felt more LA or Manhattan than Chestnut Hill. It was a level of sophistication that simply had not been available in the suburbs, and guests seemed to enjoy a true night on the town without having to take a trip into the city, with free valet parking to boot. I got exactly the broad reception that I had hoped for—at 5 p.m. I had senior citizens joining me for dinner, and at 1 a.m. I was gently ushering the thirty-year-olds out the door to continue their party elsewhere. Dinner service was brisk. People were in an optimistic frame of mind in 2005, and though we were best known for our steaks and modern take on classic food, we found that people were surprisingly willing, even eager, to venture beyond the classics when given the opportunity. Thus, Jeff could experiment with head-to-tail dishes like beef cheeks, sweetbreads, tongue, bone marrow, and all the other delicious animal bits so often ignored in this country. The economy was flush, and at our guests' request we were spooning caviar at $100 per teaspoon onto their baked potatoes and opening $500 bottles of wine.

In addition, the restaurant was situated between a cluster of hospitals and clinics and the homes where many of the doctors who worked there resided. Metropolitan Club was the perfect venue for pharmaceutical reps to wine and dine medical practitioners who were considering prescribing or recommending their drugs. That business alone grossed us about $800,000 that first year. I was relieved. We were turning out lovely food and turning a profit. And soon afterward, I received perhaps the biggest compliment possible: Capital Grille's execs started showing up at my bar. When they began making changes to their menu I realized that I had stumbled onto the cutting edge of something. People wanted steak, but they wanted more than what the usual steak house had to offer. Modernizing the old-school steak house provided a bridge between people's taste for tradition and their desire for the menu to reflect the times. I was less pleased when Capital Grille started approaching my staff, but I contained my irritation and told myself that was the price of making great hires. Besides, I had to admit that much of what I was doing right was a result of following many tenets of their blueprint for success.

The first eighteen months in a restaurant's life can be a mirage. You're packed, you're doing silly numbers, and you want to believe it will go on forever. But success is fickle. It's not that hard to get people to come check you out when you first open. The media coverage gets you a lot of initial attention and people are curious to try you for themselves. Only once the hype has died down and the novelty has worn off will you find out whether you really understand your business and have built something sustainable. As my sister once pointed out to me, you can be making $50 million, but if you're spending $51 million, you don't have a viable business. It's great to create art, but to build a successful business you've got to keep a laser focus on the commerce, too.

I had always been confident that I had the resources to guarantee the restaurant's survival for the first eighteen months. Maintaining the restaurant's success beyond that, however, would prove my mettle as a restaurateur. It wouldn't be easy. In fact, during my first week in business, the owner of the renowned Legal Sea Foods restaurant chain, Roger Berkowitz, came in to eat. He told me that he loved the place, but wondered why on earth I'd chosen such a difficult location. "If you can make it here," he said sympathetically, "you can make it anywhere."

I had no idea what he meant. I found out later, however, that Roger trained all of his staff in the Legal location in Chestnut Hill. I soon came to understand why. The clientele in Chestnut Hill is demanding and difficult. As such, it's the perfect place for a proprietor to cut her teeth. In one swift swipe of my pen on the lease, my role in the neighborhood where I grew up had changed. Before I was a neighbor, friend, and daughter. Now I was an entertainer and service provider, too, and that would make a world of difference in the way people interacted with me.

From my father and Stephi, and from my own experience working at Stephi's, I already knew that the restaurant business wasn't nearly as glamorous as it seemed. But sometimes as I changed yet another roll of toilet paper or plunged a nasty clogged toilet, I'd remember my movie days with more than a little nostalgia. Every day brought something unexpected. One thing I learned quickly is that when people drink in a crowded setting, even one as upscale as my restaurant, normally rational people can lose their minds. For all the liveliness, sometimes all it would take was one perceived slight for a fight to break out between guests. It wasn't my young patrons who caused the most trouble, either (we had a policy against sell-ing shots). The drama almost always erupted from the people you'd least expect. One night I stood agape as two friends of mine from the neighborhood, perfectly respectable people, started screaming at each other and came to fisticuffs in the lobby. A brawl damn near broke out. Of course, it was already restaurant policy to call cabs for guests who had clearly had too much to drink, but the nights when tensions ran high reminded me that my responsibility to take care of my guests went a lot further than ensuring their steaks were cooked to perfection.

I also learned that although part of the pleasure of opening a restaurant is that you become an intricate part of your com-munity, with that comes a whole other set of responsibilities and red tape. For the first time in my life, I had to pay close attention to local politics. I worked on building relationships with community leaders and started making time to attend town meetings. Yet despite my efforts, and despite the fact that I was located on a commercial street that had been a site for restaurants for years, some of my neighbors acted as though I were an invader intent on destroying their peace. At first I made it my mission to prove to them that I had only good intentions and I bent over backward to be a good neighbor and address legitimate complaints as quickly as possible. For example, as soon as I found out the sound of smashing bottles was bothering people when we took out the recycling at night, we set up a system so that all the recycling got taken out mid-morning, when people were less likely to be home. I offered the local neighbors a 20 percent discount, thinking maybe the restaurant was too pricey for them, but they flat out rejected my offer.

Nothing I did to make peace mattered. There was a core group that had decided that unless I could magically transform myself into a bank that closed at 5 p.m. every night, I would be on their hit list. Not that the area needed another bank. In fact, we were using a local bank's parking lot because it was always empty after business hours. Capital Grille offered free valet parking, which meant we had to as well, even though it was terribly expensive. No one in the neighborhood ever used that lot, but one day I was presented with a copy of the deed, dated years back, that stated the lot could be used only by neighborhood residents. Fortunately, I found another lot. But then the neighbors complained that the valet was speeding through the streets, and demanded that I hire a cop to detail every evening. This was prohibitively expensive but I did it anyway. The cop reported back that in fact the valet drove perfectly; it was the neighbors who were speeding through the neighborhood. I felt like I was the target of a witch hunt.

Every time I solved one problem, I was informed that there was another. I often wondered what these people were thinking when they bought their homes along a commercial section of Route Nine. It was no secret that it was a busy retail destination, and had been since the beginning of time. Were these people just not pro-business? Did they have too much time on their hands? A selectman would dine with us and then kowtow to his constituents in public. The politics were frustrating.

The only thing I could do was keep approaching every encounter with as much civility and good will as possible. In the end, it wasn't my excellent diplomatic skills that helped ease the tension, but simply being tenacious enough to be the last person standing. In a relatively short amount of time, most of the core group that didn't like the idea of a late-night establishment in their area moved away, and the complaints evaporated—because I wasn't the problem. It was a rough experience, and an expensive one, but like all tough obstacles, in the long run it made me a better operator. And despite the indifference with which my efforts to make peace were initially met, I will always continue to bend over backward to appease people's concerns whenever I can. Maintaining your reputation as someone who takes the high road always pays off in the end.

As much as it bothered me to know that I couldn't win everyone over, I did take comfort in knowing that the vast majority of people loved having me in their neighborhood. I knew that if I provided a fun, sexy environment, people would come to me to enjoy themselves. I just didn't count on the fact that they would also have sex. In my restaurant. Usually in the bathroom. Many times a line would form outside the bathroom until finally someone would get the attention of a manager and say, "Um, I think people are having sex in there." Or we'd be closing up and hear something, and then have to knock on the bathroom door and escort people out. I don't know why, but there's one corner of the MET Club lounge that's like our very own pornography channel (it's dark, but not quite dark enough). I guess there are some people who get off on the exhibitionism. Unless people are actually stripping off their clothes, we rarely say anything. What's there to say? These people know they're behaving inappropriately. We're more likely to speak up if someone's children are bothering other diners (though I won't ever say a word to a breastfeeding mother). People have less tolerance for kids or for screaming drunks than for a couple whose make-out session gets out of hand. My staff and I try not to get involved in other people's business unless they are threatening or hurting someone else. There are many times when we've called a cab for someone. Occasionally we've called the police. My managers have had to break up fights between exes who run into each other with their new partners and restrain a customer who insisted on flirting with a bartender by throwing popcorn and nuts at her. People can be strange and unpredictable, yet another reason why you have to hire strong management who are not afraid of conflict.

It wasn't just the guests and other outside influences that

introduced unexpected challenges. I brought plenty of them upon myself by underestimating the enormity of what I was trying to accomplish and how hard it was for other people to work according to the standards Chestnut Hill and I demanded. While I was having brunch at the Hotel Bel-Air with my cousins Wendy and Jeff, who had just moved to Los Angeles, I had an epiphany that would heavily impact the Metropolitan Club. The Bel-Air brunch menu was entirely prix fixe, yet none of us felt capable of eating a five-course meal, so although there were no a la carte options listed, we decided to ask if it was possible to order some individual dishes anyway. I was half expecting to be told no, or to at least get a little bit of attitude. This was the Bel-Air, after all. Yet whatever my cousin and I asked for, we got, followed with the word "Absolutely." I realized that the service I received at the Bel-Air was exactly what I wanted my guests to experience when they were dining in my restaurant. From then on, the Metropolitan Club was run according to the Absolutely Rule. When my guests asked for something, the waiter would not reply, "Yes." The correct answer to anything the guest asked for would always be, "Absolutely." Great hospitality is about making people believe that nothing gives you more pleasure than making them happy. My staff was under strict instructions: if you can, do. If you can't, get as close to it as possible. I was surprised to discover that this was as controversial an idea as offering diners a bar menu in addition to the regular one. Quite frankly, it drove my chefs crazy. I'd get angry when I found out they were resisting complying with certain requests. Now, I understand why the Absolutely Rule can make the lives of chefs and waiters extremely difficult. Aside from the fact that allowing, even encouraging, guests to customize every dish means that sometimes the chef has to prepare food in a way that doesn't meet his standards and can sometimes actually cause him pain—good God, lamb chops well done?—it does indeed slow down the kitchen and make the restaurant an exceedingly hard place to work. The line cooks are trained to operate their kitchen like a machine, and my policy throws a wrench in their best-laid plans almost every day. But I hold firm. If a guest asks for wasabi, and all we have is wasabi powder, somebody had better take the extra five minutes to make wasabi paste, even if it means turning the kitchen upside down to make it happen. And while I have huge respect for my chefs and their expertise, I don't actually care that it's sacrilege to cook lamb chops well done. If the guest likes overcooked lamb chops, the guest is going to get overcooked lamb chops, with a smile.

Without the Absolutely Rule I couldn't infuse my restaurants with nearly as much of that all-important "Wow" factor. Wow is about going the extra service mile. Not long ago I interviewed a waiter from another restaurant for a management job, and he told me how a customer asked for a Snapple, but his restaurant didn't sell Snapple. The market across the street did, however, so he jogged across the street, bought the Snapple, and brought it back to the table. I hope he got a tremendous tip. He got the job working for me.

Wow is agreeing to create an authentic Indian or Chinese meal for a private party, even though you're a steak house. It's about finding out that one of your bar regulars loves an esoteric scotch and making sure you have it in stock the next time she comes in. It's cooking a steak—on the bone—half medium and half rare, and then allowing the table to split and share it. These are the kinds of requests we get. We say, "Absolutely," and the guest says, "Wow!"

By now I think the residents of Chestnut Hill and I have broken everyone who works there. I can't have people working for me who don't fully embrace the idea that, to the best of our abilities, what the guest wants, the guest gets. Why am I so adamant about the Absolutely Rule? Because the way we treat the people who dine with us creates a culture for long-term success. The health of my restaurants depends on everyone who works there embracing that what-you-want-is-what-you-get philosophy.

MET Club's Favorite Black and White Cookies

Vanilla Shortbread
- 1 ½ pounds butter
- 2 cups confectioners (10-x powdered) sugar
- 1 teaspoon salt
- 1 tablespoon vanilla
- 1 15 ½ ounce package all purpose flour

Chocolate Shortbread
- 1 ½ pounds butter
- 2 cups confectioners (10-x powdered) sugar
- 1 teaspoon salt
- 1 tablespoon vanilla
- 19 ounce package all purpose flour
- 6 ounces unsweetened cocoa

Cream butter and sugar together. Add in vanilla and salt. Mix to combine, and scrape the sides of the bowl. Mix in the flour, or flour and cocoa when making the chocolate shortbread.

Roll dough between half sheets of parchment all the way to the edges, maintaining even thickness. Chill.

Lay the chocolate slab on top of the vanilla. Cut in half and flip one slab over, then layer on top of the first slab. You should now have alternating layers of vanilla and chocolate.

Cut into even strips and sandwich the strips to form a log, making sure the strips form a checkerboard pattern. Wrap tightly in parchment paper and freeze.

Cut into ¼ inch thickness. Bake at 325 degrees until the edges start to color, about 10-12 minutes.

———————————

Over the years, in fact, I have noticed even the fanciest chefs want to please. What-you-want-is-what-you-get has pervaded even the top echelons of fine dining. One night I was enjoying a globe of roasted foie gras at Per Se, Thomas Keller's extraordinary restaurant on Central Park South in New York City. As it landed on the table I casually mentioned to someone next to me that I'd love to eat this with toasted brioche and unsalted butter. Two seconds later the waiter brought me the most beautiful, fresh, hot brioche and a perfectly carved pat of butter with a little sea salt on the side. I was stunned, and so happy. It was probably one of the best dishes I have ever eaten. What does such incredible service say? Even Thomas Keller wants me to have it the way I want it.

Sometimes people take advantage. Or maybe they just get confused because the restaurant is such a social environment and they think it's all one big party. The proprietor of the El San Juan in Puerto Rico who warned me that everyone wants something for free is right. People like to feel special, and they do if you give them things for free. My bartender recently informed me that a group of regulars had told him that we weren't being as generous as Capital Grille, where they often get buy-one-get-one-free deals. I've had to be strict about our comp policy because, hey, this is a business. But I finally gave my bartenders more freedom to give comps. Bartenders drive the business; people look to bartenders to take care of them, and they need the freedom to top people off, give them free drinks, and make them feel special. They can't do their jobs well if they have to check with me every time they want to go the extra mile.

I'd like to see people's reactions if I came to their place of business and asked them to provide me with free products and services. But that's the price of business. At least, that's the price of doing business in the restaurant industry. And in the end, one hopes it pays off.

My commitment to the Absolutely Rule is challenged daily. And it was challenged most notably on opening week at my fourth restaurant, MET Back Bay, by my very own mother. I know she meant well. She was extremely supportive of my new endeavor and she was proud to show the restaurant off, which is why she showed up for lunch with nine of her friends. Every single woman at the table ordered the chopped salad, a huge, colorful mound of just about everything good my chef and I could think of, including beets, broccoli, egg, and bacon, cut into perfect, tiny cubes. Unfortunately, every single woman at the table also had very specific instructions about what we were and were not to include in her salad.

Opening week at any restaurant is fraught with trial and error as everyone works out any kinks in the system, and at that time one of our kinks was that we were having a hard time getting those chopped salads made perfectly to order. With no fewer than eighteen ingredients, it was difficult for the line to keep the recipe straight. We could barely get one salad right, let alone ten, with multiple "holds" and substitutions. I couldn't believe my own mother had done this to me—she knew very well what opening week in a restaurant was like. But in the end, the ladies got what they asked for. They may have even helped get us up to speed a bit faster than we might have otherwise. It was a good lesson. No one cared that it was opening week, they just wanted their food the way they wanted it. I couldn't let excuses get in the way of delivering on my own promise.

The fact that food is so subjective—three people at a table can have three different opinions on what qualifies as medium rare—makes it a major challenge to get things right every single time. The dining public simply has no clue how hard it is to coordinate all the moving parts required to turn out an excellent meal. Things will go wrong, and when they do, what's important is how you recover. A happy guest is a return guest. You can recover from almost any mistake if people believe that you have done your absolute best to accommodate them. Sometimes, unfortunately, your best efforts aren't enough.

Occasionally, as we found out, your best efforts are the problem. There was a couple who started coming in three times a week to the restaurant. They clearly loved the place, and they came so often we were quickly able to anticipate their preferences, such as their favorite table or their favorite drink. In another era we would have had a pair of slippers and a nicely packed pipe waiting for them upon arrival. On their 350th night in the restaurant, we brought out a bottle of Macallan scotch—the gentleman's favorite—as a gesture of gratitude for their patronage and support. After that night, we never saw them again. For weeks we tried to reach out to them to find out what we could have done to offend, but we never found out why they retreated. We thought we were doing something nice by acknowledging them, but we had obviously misunderstood. They didn't want to be noticed, and it must have made them uncomfortable to realize they were on our radar. Reading people is an excruciatingly difficult art. It is rare, however, that people don't respond positively to my staff's efforts to make them feel welcome and appreciated.

Part of Metropolitan Club's success was due to the team I had put together and the great hires we had made. When you're part of the original team that opens a new business, you share a special sense of intimacy. The restaurant business is extremely social anyway, and it's easy for people working together to start to feel like family. When someone decides they no longer want to be a part of it, it can be painful. I took it personally when a well-known pastry chef I had hired decided to move on to a different restaurant after less than a year. In fact, I was heartbroken. Not only were her desserts a major draw to the restaurant, but everyone on my staff felt essential and important to me. I was convinced that I'd never be able to replace her. After accepting her notice I went to console myself at the bar, and there I found two good friends enjoying their drinks. One of them, Ely, was a successful businessman, and after hearing why I looked so glum, he said, "Kathy, what you're building is going to be way bigger than any one person. Hopefully it will be something bigger than you. I'm going to come in here tomorrow at 5 P.M. and I had better not notice that a single thing has changed." I had gotten so wrapped up in the daily details of my business that I had completely lost sight of the fact that I was also building a brand.

Original Lemon-Lime Meringue Pie

Crust

> 2 cups all purpose flour
> 1 cup cake flour
> 1 tablespoon sugar
> 1 teaspoon salt
> 4 ounces of butter, cold
> 3 ¾ ounces shortening
> 4 ounces cold water

1. Using paddle attachment, blend all the dry ingredients together.
2. Cut in the cold butter and shortening.

3. Mix in the cold water, until all is combined, this will look a bit shaggy. Form into one mass lump with hands. Break off into 13 ounce portions and wrap well in plastic. Store in freezer until needed.

Filling:

    2 ½ cups sugar
    5 tablespoons all purpose flour
    7 ½ tablespoons cornstarch
    ½ teaspoon salt
    15 ounces water
    15 ounces milk
    3 ounces lemon juice
    1 ½ ounces lime juice
    Zest of one lemon
    5 tablespoons butter
    5 ounces egg yolk
    8 egg whites
    1 ⅓ cups sugar
    Pinch of salt

1. Whisk together the sugar, flour, salt, and cornstarch in a pot.
2. Gradually whisk in liquids to smooth.
3. Bring to a boil.
4. Add in butter.
5. Temper into yolks, return to pot and bring to a boil and thicken.
6. Pour into prebaked pie shell.
7. In mixing bowl combine whites, sugar, and salt.
8. Heat over a double boiler until 140 degrees.
9. Whip in mixer until shiny and stiff.
10. Gently spread over the pie filling—make sure to go all the way to the edges and to give it some tall peaks.
11. Bake at 325 degrees for 10-15 minutes.

12. Allow to cool at room temperature for at least on hour, chill for several hours before cutting.

Ely's words were a much-needed reminder at a critical moment, and they changed the way I looked at the business and what I was growing. I realized that if I didn't learn to toughen up and cope better with change, I was never going to be able to grow the kind of business I had been dreaming about. For the record, no one did notice that our pastry chef was gone the next day. And the experience left me better prepared when about a year after we opened, I returned from a trip to Greece to find out that my chef, Jeff Fournier, had bought a restaurant space about two miles away without telling me. I had always known that Jeff would eventually want to open his own restaurant and I would have wholeheartedly supported that decision. It was just a shock to find out he had done it without my knowledge and left me with almost no time to find a replacement for him. Enraged, I let him go on the spot. But now I had a problem. How the hell was I going to make it through dinner service the next day with no chef? And then I remembered Ely's words: Just make sure no one notices. Jeff's sous chef graciously stayed on until I found Jeff's replacement.

Jeff was a brilliant chef, but after he left I realized that he was better suited for his own chef-driven restaurant than for a large concept. When you're cooking for your own restaurant, you might be able to justify indulging in certain artistic preferences, but when you're a chef working for a business owner, the profitability of the business has to be paramount. It's hard when it's not your own place to make profitability a priority, and I think once Jeff was running his own restaurant he understood far better why I had to hold the financial reins so tightly. After he left, Carl and I were quickly able to see where we needed to get better control of food costs if we wanted to start making more money. I was grateful to have gained that perspective when I started looking for another chef. That turned out to be Todd Winer, and we have worked together ever since. (He has since become the MET Restaurant Group's Culinary Director, and now that we have more buying power thanks to our increased volume, he and my COO, Jamie Kaye, are able to negotiate deals at an extremely advantageous cost.)

My hiring technique has evolved in the seven years since I first got into the business. It's a little different when I interview someone for a management position; I ask a range of questions, some of which seemingly have nothing to do with the restaurant business, like what a candidate reads for pleasure. I ask the hard questions, but the conversation is what's important to me. I want to know more about the person who might work for me, not just more about his résumé. I also ask a lot of hypotheticals. One thing that is important to me is to know where people naturally gravitate, where they feel most comfortable. Some managers like positioning themselves near the bar; some are brilliant at the host stand greeting guests, some love being in the kitchen, expediting. Their preferences tell me a lot about how they will likely work in the restaurant. I'll set up a scenario: it's a busy Saturday night and there are two hundred covers on the books and you're running a half hour late at the host stand, your kitchen is in the weeds, your bar is slammed, what do you do? Their answers—who they choose to help, where they choose to go first—helps me determine who they are and whether their strengths complement what I already have on staff. Building upon people's complementary strengths is the key to building any solid business team.

Experience is important, but it isn't always the first thing I look for when I'm adding someone new to my leadership team. I want to hire people who are curious and energetic and who are willing to learn, who are natural at being gracious, who know how to put the capital "H" in Hospitality. You'd be amazed at how many people in this industry have no idea what hospitality really looks like, nor do they care. I also think that fun is infectious, and certain people exude it and others don't. I want to be around people who know how to have fun and impart that sense to the rest of their team. There's nothing worse than going into a place where everyone is scowling. You can have a delicious meal or cocktail, but if your waiter or bartender is surly, or snobby, or impatient, that's what you'll remember, not the lovely meal or drink, and you'll be unlikely to return. I want to hire people who are able to put their egos aside and execute my vision. I want people whose personalities will mesh with the rest of my staff, and whose energy will add a sense of fun and exuberance to the dining room. And I want talent. Lots of raw talent. Unfortunately, some of the most talented people can also be the most difficult to work with. Bob Kraft, owner of the New England Patriots football team, gave me some advice early on: if you've got someone brilliant on your team, but he's a turkey, get rid of him. He'd seen it time and time again with the Patriots, where he'd have a phenomenally talented player who was simply such a loose cannon, distracting and disruptive to the rest of the team, that he had to be cut.

I have a hard time being that draconian. As a woman, I bring a lot of my maternal instincts to the job. I expect people to be exceedingly committed to what we are building but I'm respectful of the fact that people have personal lives. Life goes by so quickly, and people have to connect with their partner and their mother and their siblings. I'm not sure male business owners are quite as cognizant of that fact, and if they are, I'm not sure many would allow it to temper their business decisions.

But I don't think my approach makes me soft. People are better employees when they know they are respected, and that their life away from work matters, too. This is why I will soon be implementing new vacation policy that grants people three weeks of paid vacation after working for me for three years, and a month of vacation once they've worked for five years at the company. When people work for me they work hard and they work long hours, and I think it's only fair that I give back with more than just a paycheck. Do I live by this philosophy because I'm a woman or because I'm progressive? I'm not sure, but I do probably care more than most male bosses do about quality of life issues and whether people are happy at work and at home.

I rely heavily on my intuition, and I believe in giving people second chances. You can't change people, but you can guide them to making smarter choices. The restaurant business is filled with young people who are still testing their wings; if I can help someone achieve her full potential by giving her a second chance, it's to her benefit but it's also to mine and the business's. Finding and keeping a staff that will feel invested in your business is one of the greatest challenges to running a restaurant, and I have found that the only way to encourage that sense of ownership is to let them know that you are invested in them, too. Figuring out which wild horses you can break and which ones you can't is one of the best skills a restaurateur can learn, and could possibly be my biggest weakness.

Todd was a wild stallion. He had it all—talent, ambition, an interest in being part of a growing business, and experience. In fact, he had worked for nine years with Todd English (though not in the space I had taken over), opening many of his restaurants in the United States and abroad. But he also had a working style that conflicted with my more nurturing philosophy. I don't believe you lead by intimidation, I believe you lead by inspiration. He had learned his trade in the old-school Gordon Ramsay model of pounding his fists and throwing pans. I do not allow my team to swear at each other. It took a while, but in the end Todd softened his management approach, and we've become a strong team.

Though chefs and owners are similarly focused on doing what is in the best interest of the restaurant, the dynamic between the two can be difficult. The chef is team captain and as such is in charge of the kitchen, but it is the owner who raises the money, gives birth to the concept, and, in my case at least, writes many of the menus, so the chef is playing with the owner's ball and bat and on her field. Last summer, my mom, Carl, and I went back to visit old man Cipriani at his still magical restaurant Harry's Bar, overlooking the grand canals of Venice. We ate those perfect ham sandwiches that are not on the menu (Carl and I went back two nights in a row just for those) and, of course, the green noodles in cream sauce, flecked with ham and covered with cheese.

Obviously, my first time there at the age of thirteen I had no idea that one day Arrigo Cipriani would share prophetic words with me as a fellow business owner. I had been back many times through the years but this time Arrigo sat down with us and told us a story about Harry's opening. The very first chef they hired, they fired, because his ego was so preposterous that he filled his kitchen not with other chefs, but with excellent cooks. That's when Arrigo realized that it was he who was running the restaurant, not some ill-tempered, ego-driven maniac who didn't have the restaurant's best interest at heart. It must be hard to work as a chef when the concept is bigger than you, but if you can't take pride and pleasure in making something big happen and being part of that, this isn't the kind of business environment for you. There is nothing wrong with being an excellent cook. It may be the biggest compliment of all.

For the relationship to work well, it's essential that both

chef and owner treat the other with respect, and to instinctively know when to push back and when to accede. I believe that's why Todd and I work so well together. I'm no slouch in the kitchen, but Todd is exceedingly talented and has an exceptional palate. There are few people I would rather share a meal with, and as much as I know about food he can still manage to surprise me. Todd honed his craft working alongside the tremendously successful and talented Todd English. But English, as much as I love him, is a better chef than businessman, so Todd often defers to me in practical business matters.

With Todd I found the kind of working relationship that in many ways I had missed from my movie days. He has done a remarkable job of interpreting my vision. Jeff's work was visually stunning; he could turn a plate into a canvas using Peruvian potatoes and turnips and carrots. But though his plating was beautiful, it never actually felt like a perfect fit for what I was trying to convey with Metropolitan Club. There was, quite simply, too much Jeff on the plate. In his restaurant, that is exactly how it should be. But not in mine. It was a good lesson for me, and from that time on I was always careful to hire chefs who understood how to temper their own vision with mine. It takes enormous talent to be able to do that well, and very rarely does Todd miss.

Around 2008 the world started to financially implode, and it didn't take long to feel the impact. We had started out high-end, going head to head with Capital Grille with our modern steak house, and we had succeeded beyond my greatest hope. But all of a sudden, our numbers started to shift. Orders for escargot and prime rib plummeted, and no one was ordering expensive bottles of wine anymore. Talk of recession had people understandably spooked, and they were starting to look for ways to cut back on their expenses, the easiest of which was eliminating meals out, or at least downgrading them to more casual fare. Despite my affordable bar menu, I was still perceived as expensive, and it was starting to hurt me. It was time to make some changes.

The year 2008 marked a major turning point in the way I ran the business. Our top-line sales started to drop. We were feeling the effects of the slipping economy but the damage was exacerbated when Massachusetts passed a law prohibiting pharmaceutical reps from giving gifts, such as nice dinners, to the doctors they were wooing. We took a huge hit when we lost that business. Strong top-line sales can hide a multitude of sins, but without all that revenue coming in Carl and I were able to see much more clearly where there was waste and excess. You find out just how good an operator you really are if you can keep making money even though you're not bringing in as much revenue as you had been. It's hard to tighten that belt, but if doesn't kill you, it makes you a whole lot stronger.

Fortunately, I had taken a conservative approach when setting up my financial plan. Certainly, when you're courting investors or otherwise projecting numbers, you have to be optimistic. But you have to be fiscally responsible, too. I never assumed that our sales would increase every year, and Carl and I had our Aloha point of sale system set up to keep an eagle eye on our expenses. Like other restaurants, we relied on the PMIX reports it generated to tell us what guests were eating and drinking, so that we could see where there was waste and quickly adjust our orders. But Carl and I took all the rest of the information we could glean from the system, as well as from Open Table, to create additional reports and spreadsheets that were mind blowing in their detail and scope. By scrutinizing these reports every day, we could see when we were making money, during what hours, and what we were spending money on besides food and drink. We could analyze cover counts versus sales at different times of the day, and then compare them from day to day, week to week, or month to month. We also created charts to give us a clear idea of trends in the restaurant.

For example, we could see how the volume at the bar ebbed and flowed on any given night. Was Tuesday night at the bar consistently busy? Did we really need two bartenders and three cocktail servers, or would one bartender and two servers suffice? As soon as you see your sales go down and your labor costs go up, you know you have to make hard decisions about who and what to cut. Mining our POS system and building our own spreadsheets so we can extrapolate the data allowed us to manage our labor and our costs quickly and adeptly, so that we were in a good position to weather the coming recession, and to make adjustments wherever necessary.

Not everyone loves my obsession with numbers (actually, it's Carl's obsession...I'm just smart enough to reap the benefits of his phenomenally detail-oriented mind). The managers and executives at my company have to fill out more paperwork in more detail than employees at some of the biggest corporate businesses in the world. We require that kind of detailed accountability so that we can respond immediately when something isn't working. We struggle with a catch-22—we want our managers on the floor, not stuck in the office doing paperwork, but at the same time the paperwork is essential to our survival. A lot of big companies have set up satellite accounting departments so that their managers don't have to deal with the paperwork. But I think that removes managers too far away from the actual business of restaurants. If our managers understand the numbers well, they can effectively problem solve and run the business.

As it turned out, the changes I felt compelled to make in response to the recession ultimately turned out to be great improvements. For example, the bar had always felt a little overwhelming; the architect had left too much empty space between the bar and the banquette. Lately, there was a wait to eat in the bar because people increasingly wanted to eat there rather than in the dining room. Part of that was the casual atmosphere and part of it was psychological—it just feels like you're spending less time and less money when you're eating in a bar than when you're sitting down at a table, even though most of the time, you're not. A restaurateur has to make as much money as possible every day, and you can only do as much business as you have seats. So the solution to the space issue and my decreasing profit was to add more seats in the bar. I added a row of high tops between the bar and the banquette, and I replaced the single table in front of the fireplace with four more high tops. Seats track to dollars. The seats filled exponentially at the bar, and my numbers went up. Most importantly, the additional seats gave the bar a cozier feel and made it an even nicer place for people to hang out and enjoy themselves. That, too, certainly helped business.

I was concerned that making changes to the menu and offering dishes at a value would be perceived as a sign that we were in trouble. Offering a "deal" without tarnishing your brand means walking a very fine line. We had all sorts of internal discussions about the wording we would use so that we could show we were sensitive to the changing times yet not scream fire sale. We didn't want to follow Capital Grille, which had started giving appetizers away for free at their bar. Interestingly, when I spoke to the general manager at Cap Grille about it, he told me that patrons were coming to his restaurant for the free apps and then heading over to MET Club to drink. In addition, it was the same people coming night after night; the tactic wasn't drawing any new business.

So we reluctantly set about making important changes to the menu to highlight the value we could provide and counteract our image as an expensive place to eat. I started selling specials each night of dishes we were known for. Monday was burger night at $4.99. Then we started Taco Tuesdays. Wednesday night was a two-for-one lobster special (in my neck of the woods, people will drive a long way for a twofer on lobster). Thursday night, steak and fries. I did my best to let people know how much I appreciated that, when they were making the decision about where to spend their hard-earned money, they had chosen us. The specials were an instant hit and they have become a permanent part of our repertoire.

Unfortunately, no matter how hard we tried to keep our numbers up by adjusting the menu and the seating capacity, we still had to let staff go. That was extremely tough. It would be wise if everyone ran a bare-bones business right from the start to avoid having to lay anyone off later, but that's hard to do. The house needs to get unexpectedly slammed just once for you to realize that having too few people on deck can be as disastrous as having too many. Once you cut out the fat, though, you realize what you can live without. When business is going well it's easy to carry a lot of padding and not notice it. It's only when sales start to fall that you realize you've got too many hosts, too many people on the line, and busboys without enough to do. A restaurateur is always walking a fine line between encouraging a sense of conviviality and team spirit by trying to accommodate the forty-hour weeks most employees want to work and yet remembering that every staff member represents labor costs. In order to keep good people you have to pay close attention to their hours, which translates to their being able to pay their rent and support their lives. I have always felt you are better off with one strong, talented person rather than two or three mediocre ones. What one solid person can accomplish in a 40-hour week is close to a miracle. I am always looking to identify and reward those talented, passionate people. However, when labor costs overextend your budget, it's time to make tough decisions. Those moments when I've had to let people go have been some of the most painful of my career.

In the midst of the most devastating financial crisis the country has faced since the Great Depression, it might have seemed like I would have been wise to focus on my restaurant and put off any plans of expanding. But in truth, the reason I was able to adjust so quickly to the changing economic tide was that I had predicted the downturn all along, as well as its subsequent jolt to the restaurant world. And as I made plans to shore up my existing restaurant, I had seen an opportunity in the midst of all the doom and gloom, and had quietly started taking the steps necessary to bring it to life.

Eight

Writing My Own Recipe for Success

Of all the foods that can summon back the days of my childhood, and clearly there are many, none is as evocative as a hamburger. To me, a perfectly grilled burger is the taste of happiness, safety, family, tenderness, and love. It tastes of the days my sister and I spent in Switzerland on winter holiday, when Dad would rouse us out of bed at the crack of dawn to make sure we were out on the slopes before anyone else could track the powder from the previous night's snowfall. After long days of skiing, he would take us to eat at any one of a number of charming Swiss restaurants. We'd be ravenous after all that exercise, and would throw ourselves on our food with gusto, gorging on spaghetti Bolognese (my dad's favorite), Hobelkase, Gemischter salad, all-you-could-eat roasted baby goat at the local train station in Saanen, crispy rosti, and of course, raclette, which was sometimes melted from the heat of a roaring fire and scraped straight from a wheel onto your plate. A meal that stands out most in my mind, however, occurred in a little stubli, a Swiss-style pub, in Saanen. The pub had a charcoal pit where they cooked fabulous steaks and burgers.

It was here that I tasted my first farm burger, a plump patty covered with Gruyere cheese and married to a farm-fresh fried egg. Unbeknownst to me at the time, that very burger would become the genesis for my second restaurant concept. That is when I had the revelation that a burger could be a canvas for an endless number of taste and texture combinations.

For a family that took pride in its adventurous palate, we ate a surprising number of hamburgers. Every Saturday was burger day in our home. It was the one afternoon a week when Dad would cook for the family. His specialty was a Dagwood, a double burger sandwich with all the fixings. I would sit near him and watch him hand form the freshly ground beef as delicately as pastry dough. The trick to a perfect burger, he would remind my sister and me, was to buy meat with a high fat-to-beef ratio, and then handle it very little, patting the meat into shape as quickly as possible. For seasoning, he'd use nothing more than a generous sprinkle of kosher salt and ground black pepper. He would stoke the coals under the grill with all the care and intensity of a warlock tending his cauldron, until the embers were red-hot and the thick iron bars smoked. The meat would hit the metal with a loud, searing hiss as a charred protective crust formed around the luscious, creamy interior. He made a point of touching the burger only once with the spatula, to flip it. At the last minute, he'd toss a heavily buttered bun onto the grill.

My job was to make our family's special sauce, which was really just a homemade Russian dressing made up of Hellmann's mayonnaise, Heinz ketchup, sweet piccalilli relish, and a touch of Dijon. There were always many cheeses to choose from, as we each had our preference; I have always been a cheddar girl myself. Finally, we'd start to build our works of art, layering each burger with Boston lettuce, ripe tomato, and a thick slice of red onion. As we each took our first bite of our masterpieces, all conversation would stop. Not much tastes better than the earthy, rich steak flavor of a charcoal-grilled burger, and a burger cooked by Dad on a warm spring Saturday afternoon was pure heaven.

As much as we loved the farm burgers and the Saturday Dagwoods, though, none of us was above exclaiming with joy at the sight of a pair of golden arches rising to greet us as we returned home from a family drive or a sail. Our orders were mundane—a Big Mac or Quarter Pounder with fries—but we got creative with our beverages, ordering one coffee shake and one chocolate shake, then mixing them together to make a sophisticated mocha.

Mawing a Quarter Pounder in the front seat of my Dad's convertible and washing it down with a mocha shake; sinking my teeth into our Saturday burgers at home; the satisfaction of a bite of pit-fired burger oozing with egg yolk after a day of rigorous exercise—these are the happy moments that cemented my lifelong love affair with burgers, and what I was probably unconsciously trying to recreate when I conceived of my second restaurant in 2006.

Within months of opening Metropolitan Club I was fielding requests from as far away as London and Singapore to open a second restaurant, mostly from big restaurant groups hoping I could recreate the MET Club magic for them in one of their new high-end developments. One of the earliest and most tempting opportunities came from Sheldon Gordon, the developer who built the phenomenally successful Forum Shops at Caesar's Palace in Las Vegas. Word of my restaurant spread among those in the know, and one of Sheldon's partners' ex-wives, who lived in Chestnut Hill, called Sheldon and told him that he had to come down and see the restaurant. So Sheldon and his entourage boarded a private plane and came in for lunch.

Sheldon Gordon had to have been eighty years old, but as soon as he walked through my door I fell a little bit in love with him. He was charismatic, charming, and as passionate about food as I. I admired what he had done with the Forum Shops, and we had eaten at many of the same places, and over a delicious lunch we bonded over our shared stories. He insisted that I come to Atlantic City the following week to see his newest and biggest project, the Pier Shops at Caesar's Palace, a giant, 300,000-square-foot, four-story mall on the water. I accepted. It was a brilliant concept to put a retail pier out on the Atlantic City boardwalk.

I got to Atlantic City and stayed at the newly renovated Caesar's Palace, trying to imagine opening my next restaurant there. A lot of people I respected were coming on board, including Stephen Starr, whose restaurants had helped do for Philadelphia what my father had done for Boston, and Todd English. I thought, "I've only been open six months and I'm being offered this!" Surely I would be crazy to turn down an opportunity that had come to me so easily. And yet, once I returned home I realized that I was so flattered by the invitation to join such a prestigious project that I was forgetting to look at this as a business deal.

As soon as I took my emotions and ego out of the equation, the answer was clear. First of all, there was no nonstop flight from Boston to Atlantic City, and it was too far for most people to drive down for the weekend. The mean income of the year-round residents around Atlantic City meant that the local demographic wasn't going to make my place a neighborhood fixture. And most important, as lovely as it is on the Jersey Shore, I didn't want to be stuck on the third floor of a pier jutting out into the ocean on a beach where it's cold nine months out of the year. That would give me very few months in which to make the bulk of my money. If I could have come up with a reason to go in other than the marquis branding opportunity I might have ignored my reservations and gone forward. I think part of the reason I wanted to work with Sheldon Gordon so badly was that he reminded me a lot of my father, and he probably could have swayed my decision had he tried hard enough. Fortunately, he didn't. It would have probably dug an early grave for the MET Club. I still consider turning that offer down to be one of the smartest things I've ever done. The best business decisions are sometimes the ones in which you say "no."

Another of the interesting opportunities that came my way lay much closer to home. Robin Brown, credited with turning the Four Seasons Boston into the city's first five-star hotel and restaurant during his years as general manager, was a frequent guest at Metropolitan Club. He was preparing to break ground on a luxury hotel and condominium, The Residences at Mandarin Oriental. Catering to Boston's rich and powerful with amenities like private elevators, a spa, and concierge service, apartments would run as high as $12 million, and hotel guests could expect to drop about $700 a night. The project was only in its infancy in 2005, but had already created tremendous buzz around the city. When Robin approached me to ask whether I would consider opening my next restaurant at the Mandarin Oriental, I was flattered.

My chef at the time, Jeff Fournier, and I met with Robin, and the meeting went well, with a surprise highlight. As Robin was praising MET Club, he added that if we were to do business together we would have to change some things about our approach. The last time he'd been in, he'd asked the waiter to make a substitution to a dish, and the waiter replied that he couldn't accommodate that request, the chef would only serve the dish prepared his way. If we were to open at Mandarin Oriental, we would have to understand that whatever the guest wanted, the guest would get. I smiled to myself. This was the have-it-your-way philosophy I had been stressing to Jeff and all of my team, and it had been a tough battle. It meant a great deal to me that Robin, the master of hospitality, confirmed that this was the standard to which the best aspired.

Robin envisioned a fancier version of the MET, a white

tablecloth restaurant. Yet as fun as it would have been to be a part of one of the most prestigious real estate deals in Boston, everything I was seeing around town and in my own restaurant was telling me that the public's mood was shifting and that the future lay in casual dining. Part of being a smart businessperson is knowing how to stand firm in the intoxicating flurry of your success. It's so easy to get carried away by the rewards of a successful business venture—the accolades, the thrill of being pursued, the money—and allow them to shift your priorities. By the end of my meeting with Robin Brown, I knew that I would turn him down. But I've always been grateful for the small gift of validation Robin gave me that day.

With MET Club I had hit on the perfect sweet spot by turning a high-quality spotlight on everyday food and bringing a little glamour to the burbs with a boutique venue. My instinct told me to keep going in that direction. I had always thought that it would be fun to do something even more commercial—a sophisticated version of McDonald's with higher-quality, modern ingredients, a place that catered to an adult demographic that would delight in retro-inspired frosty martinis and liquored-up shakes. In addition to serving a simplified version of the MET Club menu—thick steaks, specialty sandwiches, fish, and pastas, grill room food, if you will—I'd take McDonald's what-you-want-is-what-you-get ethos to a whole new level with the addition of a burger bar. Driven by the infinite possibilities available if I continued to take my inspiration from the word "Metropolitan," I decided to name my burgers after continental and international cities and create unique flavor and texture combinations using those locales' indigenous flavors. My daughter, who was now attending Brown, and I had fun one night brainstorming to develop the menus. A twist on a classic American combination such as a burger topped with mushrooms, sautéed onions, and Swiss cheese would become the Manhattan; the Dallas would have blue cheese and barbecue sauce crowned with onion rings; and the all-American DC burger would be represented by your classic cheeseburger toppings.

I would also use unusual and even exotic toppings to create fabulous, creative hamburgers with international flavor, including my version of that unbelievable Swiss farm burger topped with a fried egg, which I ultimately named the Boston Burger, but also the Paris Burger with Brie, truffle mayo, and caramelized onion. Rome—Taleggio and Bolognese! Barcelona—Serrano ham and tapenade! To top the whole experience off, I'd offer all the fixings a la carte for people to mix and match as they chose. The entire burger menu would be customizable. The whole thing sounded like so much fun to me, and made so much sense. Americans consume about fourteen billion burgers a year, 65 percent of those away from home. Very few concepts, however, gave their guests the option of making their own, their way. I loved the idea of giving them the chance to try.

MET Bar & Grill's Top-Selling Burgers

Manhattan Burger

> 1 each patty (salmon, veggie, MET, Kobe, or turkey)
> 1 each bun (sesame or 7 grain)
> 2 slices cooked bacon
> 1 each pickle spear
> 1 slice Swiss cheese
> 1 ounces caramelized onions
> 1 ounces sautéed mushrooms
> Kosher salt

1. Place the patty on the grill and season with kosher salt.
2. Cook patty to desired temperature.

3. Butter the bun and toast in the toaster.
4. When the burger is nearing the desired temperature, top it with the cheese and place the burger under the cheese melter.
5. When cheese is melted place the patty on top of the bottom bun.
6. Top the burger with the caramelized onions, mushrooms and bacon.

BURGER BUNS

> 3 ounces fresh yeast
> 3 cups milk, warmed
> 3 ounces corn oil (volume)
> 4 ½ ounces honey (volume)
> 3 eggs
> 3 pounds, 2 ounces all purpose flour
> ¾ ounces salt

1. Bloom yeast with warmed milk.
2. Add in additional ingredients and mix with dough hook on low speed for 5 minutes.
3. Cover with plastic and allow to double in size.
4. Portion and shape in ball and place on sheet pan with parchment.
5. Proof and egg wash. Sprinkle with sesame seeds.
6. Bake at 325 for 5 min, turn 5 min more.

Tokyo Burger
Makes four

> 32 ounces fresh ground Kobe beef
> 4 slices Muenster cheese, about 2 ounces each
> 4 ounces sticky soy*

1 avocado

12 ounces Kaiware sprouts

12 ounces pickled onion (24 hour prep time)*

6 ounces wasabi mayo

Wasabi Mayo

Mix 2 cups mayo with ¼ cup of wasabi paste. Then add ⅓ cup simple syrup.

Form into 8 ounce patties

*Sticky Soy Glaze

½ liter light salt soy

¼ liter orange juice fresh

1 cup lime juice fresh

1 each fresh ginger chopped

2 each chopped garlic

1 ½ each jalapeno chopped, no seeds

2 bunches cilantro

1 each Lemongrass cleaned and bruised

Corn starch slurry

Add all ingredients together bring to boil then reduce heat and simmer for 15 to 20 minutes, strain and cool.

*Pickled onions

1 red beet cut into 6 pieces

1 white onion sliced very thin

3 cups rice wine vinegar

½ cup sugar

4 cups water

Bring water, sugar, and rice wine vinegar to a boil with the beet. Place in a bowl and add sliced onions. Cover and let stand for 24 hours.

Follow steps 1-5 of the Manhattan Burger.
To assemble, brush burger with sticky soy, top with 2
tablespoons pickled onions, sprouts, and cheese. Spread bun
evenly with wasabi mayo and avocado.

Boston Burger
- 1 each patty (salmon, veggie, MET, Kobe, or turkey)
- 1 each bun (sesame or 7 grain)
- 2 slices cooked bacon
- 1 each pickle spear
- 1 each fried egg
- 1 slice cheddar cheese
- Kosher salt

Follow steps 1-5 of the Manhattan burger.
Top the burger with the fried egg and bacon.

Paris Burger
- 1 each patty (salmon, veggie, MET, Kobe, or turkey)
- 1 each bun (sesame or 7 grain)
- 1 each pickle spear
- 1 each fried egg
- 1 ounce caramelized onion
- 1 ounce Brie cheese
- 1 tablespoon truffle mayo
- Kosher Salt

Follow steps 1-5 of the Manhattan burger.
Top burger with caramelized onions and fried egg.

Rome Burger

Follow steps 1-5 of the Manhattan burger.
Top with Famous MET Bolognese Sauce.

Famous MET Bolognese
6-8 servings

2 tablespoon vegetable oil

4 tablespoons butter, divided

4 cloves of garlic slivered

2 ½ cups finely diced onion

1 cup finely diced celery

1 cup finely diced carrot

1 pound ground beef chuck

1 pound ground veal

1 pound ground pork

Salt

Fresh ground black pepper

1 cup half and half

Red pepper flakes

Parmigiano-Reggiano both grated cheese and rind

1 cup dry white wine

2 cups canned imported Italian plum tomatoes, torn into pieces, with juice

2 pounds pasta (preferably spaghetti), cooked and drained

Freshly grated Parmigiano-Reggiano cheese at the table

1. Put pancetta in pan and render. Add oil and butter and chopped onion in a heavy 3 ½-quart pot and turn heat to medium. Add slivered garlic. Cook and stir onion until it has become translucent, then add chopped celery and carrot. Cook for about 2 minutes, stirring vegetables to coat well.

2. Add ground beef, pork, veal, and a large pinch of salt and a few grindings of pepper and a pinch of red pepper flakes. Crumble meat with a fork, stir well and cook until beef has lost its raw, red color.

3. Add half and half and let simmer gently, stirring frequently, until it has bubbled away completely. Add a pinch of fresh nutmeg and stir.
4. Add wine and let it simmer until it has evaporated. Add tomatoes and stir thoroughly to coat all ingredients well. When tomatoes begin to bubble, turn heat down so that sauce cooks at a slow simmer.
5. Cook, uncovered, for 3 hours or more, stirring from time to time. When finished, the liquid should evaporate and the fat should separate from the sauce. Taste and correct for salt.
6. Add remaining tablespoon butter to the hot pasta and toss with the sauce. Serve with freshly grated Parmesan on the side.

———————

My father taught me everything I needed to know about the perfect burger. The only way to keep a burger juicy is to keep your hands and spatula off of it for as long as possible. The bun should be thickly slathered with butter before you throw it on the grill. Charcoal is best (though we have to cook ours on griddles because it's faster that way). Patties should be thick— our 7.5-ounce patty is more dome than patty, because you want to be able to get a big, satisfying bite of meat. The meat-to-fat ratio is critical. Our prime blend has a custom meat-to-fat ratio that gives our burger the perfect mouthfeel and flavor yet doesn't take forever to cook. The bun-to-burger ratio also matters enormously. Too much bun and all you taste is bread; too little and it's not satisfying. And the bread has to be thick enough to hold up to the burger so that the bottom doesn't soak through and leave you holding a drippy, soggy mess instead of a sandwich. Toppings should be "coast to coast," meaning every inch of bread should be covered with your sauce, tomato, lettuce, and whatever other toppings you've included on the burger, so that every bite includes the same confluence of flavors and textures. That's a MET Rule. I relish the combination of crunchy, cool, spicy, sweet, and smoky, the ultimate flavors and textures required to achieve that blow-away burger satisfaction.

When I had chosen the name "Metropolitan" for my first restaurant, I had hoped to imply that guests could have a transformative experience there. It wasn't until Ali and I worked on our globally influenced menu, however, that I realized that the word also implied that guests could be transported. The world is small, and foreign places aren't so far away anymore. The Metropolitan concept reflected that. Even so, it took me a little while to hit on the right name for my new restaurant. I played around with several variations of "burger bar," but it was my lawyer who pointed out the obvious: "Everybody calls you the MET Bar, Kathy, so just call it the MET Bar & Grill." Of course. You know you can get a burger at a burger bar, but you don't know you can get a steak. A grillroom is far more inclusive—you can get burgers and steaks. And the bar...well, naturally I wanted to highlight the bar. Open the door, fall into the bar. Every time.

Hamburgers were a logical progression from the steak house concept and a natural extension of the brand I was building as the place to turn when you wanted a high-quality meat-centric meal. And I thought I knew exactly where such a meal might be in high demand. A major renovation and expansion was being planned for a large mall in Natick, about fifteen miles outside of Boston, and the owners, General Growth Properties, were looking for new tenants. The mall, originally called Natick Mall, was being rebranded as a high-end retail destination, as evidenced by its new name, the Natick Collection, and the establishment of two new upscale anchors, Neiman Marcus and Nordstrom.

This project intrigued me. Unlike the Atlantic City retail venue, which would only attract the demographic for my restaurant during the summer months, a luxury mall would attract them year round. A mall location would also fulfill many of the requirements I had already established for the kind of restaurant that comprised a growth business. It could accommodate a large number of seats, it had outdoor seating and private dining, and it was located in a heavily populated area that attracted lots of traffic. Be visible, and you've already won half your battle. From our seats at the McDonald's on the south side of Route One, where my family would stop on the way home from Boston after a day on the water, we had a view of another McDonald's, located directly across the highway to capture the business going in the other direction. Whether heading east or west, a hungry traveler couldn't miss these restaurants. Say what you will about McDonald's, it was a brilliant real estate maneuver.

I'd like to think that the spirit of Ray Kroc nodded in approval when he saw how I took his lesson to heart by transforming a travel agency's flat façade into Metropolitan Club's attention-grabbing corner, and then made the decision to put my next restaurant in a shopping mall. Best of all, because few people would expect to find such a nice restaurant at a mall, there was an inherent "Wow" factor built in. I knew the concept could work because Ned Grace, whose Capital Grille had helped inspire Metropolitan Club, had already done something similar. His RARE Hospitality also ran a chain of restaurants called LongHorn Steakhouse. LongHorn restaurants were located in significantly more commercial areas than their fancier cousin Capital Grille. I thought my upscale mass-market concept would be a perfect fit for Natick Collection shoppers eager for a lunch or dinner option beyond the food court.

The more I thought about all the possibilities inherent in such an idea, the more excited I became. Now I had to get my ideas on paper so I would have something to show potential investors. I had great help from an unexpected source, a young guy named Chase Chavin, who had visited MET Club during his second year at Harvard with a bunch of friends who loved hunting down great steak houses. Afterward he contacted me and asked if I would participate in a study he was conducting for Harvard Business School. He was interested in analyzing the business—steak house food costs, their gross, their net, their overall operations. I agreed, thinking it would be an interesting study and also that it was nice to do this student a favor. Not long afterward, as I was starting to put ideas together for MET Bar & Grill, I found myself frequently traveling back and forth to Chicago to see my son perform in plays through the summer acting program he was attending at the well-regarded Cherubs program at Northwestern. Chase was also in Chicago, and Carl suggested I meet him and discuss whether he would help me write my business plan. I thought it was a great suggestion. I figured I could use all the help I could get. Over the next few weeks Chase came to Boston several times and together we solidified my business objectives and developed a comprehensive list of the people who might be interested in helping the business grow.

The last time I had written a business plan was with Steve Wax at Chelsea Pictures, but this time it was just me on the line. I had run copious numbers when planning for MET Club, but since I didn't have to sell my idea to anyone to raise money, I didn't do a business plan per se. That may have been a mistake. As I discovered, writing a business plan is a great exercise. It forced me to crystallize my brand and what I wanted to build, to think into the future and develop a strategy. As I worked on my business plan for the Natick Collection, I realized that writing one for MET Club might have forced me to ask and answer some important questions ahead of time, thus sparing me some of the stress I'd suffered and helping me to prepare for some things I didn't understand until I was in the thick of operating the restaurant.

Now I needed to raise money, though, and the business plan was a great tool for explaining to investors my hopes for the company and what we wanted to do. The business plan helped me articulate my core philosophy and everything I had learned about how to build my brand. It allowed me to outline why people were responding to what I had to offer, and how I intended to recreate that magic in my second restaurant and grow the business, offering as many details as possible, down to marketing ideas and the resources I'd use. I don't know that the business plan made the process of opening in the Natick Collection any easier than when we'd opened in Chestnut Hill—it certainly didn't make it any cheaper, because opening in Natick cost a fortune–but by the time we did I had a much stronger grasp on the value of the brand and how to capital-ize on it. Plans are fantastic blueprints, though they necessarily shift as you move forward and confront challenges, obstacles, and new opportunities. Best of all, they encourage you to be proactive instead of reactive.

Asking for money to open the restaurant in Natick was one of the hardest things I have ever done. I had never had to do it before—I opened MET Club by pooling my own money with money from my family. My father had been able to help my sister round up investors when she opened her restaurant, but by the time I decided to expand my business to Natick he couldn't do it to the same degree. He certainly tried his hardest and did bring in a few people, but he wasn't the dynamo he had been years earlier. It was a huge life lesson for me to see this man, once so powerful and connected, so diminished in many ways. Aging is not easy. My father wasn't well, and illness doesn't encourage friendships, although people still had great respect for him. I think he understood what was happening to him, and it was excruciating to watch. But even from the sidelines he rooted for me, taking pride in every dollar I raised. He wanted so badly for me to have a chance.

During that time I became aware that my days with my dad were numbered. This led me to two realizations: one, I needed to spend as much time with him as possible, which I did; and two, he wasn't always going to be there, so if I was going to make this business work I'd have to be ready to do it on my own. I was almost fifty years old, and I was finally growing up.

The process of raising money for the restaurant was humbling yet liberating. If I could raise the money, it would mean people believed in my idea and believed in me. I was learning the meaning of true independence, and it was a powerful feeling.

As I prepared to seek out investors, my brother-in-law asked me whether I had perfected my sales pitch. Sales pitch? He had been an extremely successful lawyer and a marketing genius. I wasn't a salesperson—did I need a pitch? He suggested that I position the deal as an investment opportunity, not a request for help. It was a subtle but helpful piece of advice. I had fallen into an unfortunately typical female habit of underestimating what I had to offer the world. My brother-in-law's advice helped me shift my perspective just enough to realize that I wasn't asking for any favors—I had something valuable that people should want to be a part of. With that wind in my sail, I set out, knowing that it wouldn't be easy. My practical and experienced dad had warned me, "For every ten to twenty people, you'll be lucky if you get one to sign the check." I wasn't just angling for financial backing; rather, I was hoping to build a group of successful people on whom I could count for advice and support. I wanted people to be on my team. I wanted them to believe in my idea as much as I did and to help me grow it. If I couldn't find enough individual investors to help me, I'd find some other way. But I'd get that money, by hook or by crook.

Chase and I looked everywhere for potential investors, from California to Chicago. We also searched in our own backyard. A number of well-known sports figures from the New England Patriots and Boston Red Sox lived in Chestnut Hill, as did some of Boston's most prominent businesspeople, and some had become Metropolitan Club regulars. As it turned out, several were interested in helping me grow the business. They invested in the MET Brand, and would remain passive, with no decision-making power I was overwhelmed by the sense of validation I experienced after getting such a resounding vote of confidence from people in my own community.

Some people questioned my decision to open in a mall, and I still get flak for it. It certainly made the restaurant community look at me differently. Chestnut Hill was already considered a little far from the downtown scene, but at least MET Club had a boutique feel. We won *Boston Magazine's* "Best of Boston" award for Best Steakhouse in 2005, and it didn't hurt that around the time we opened, Laurent Tourondel, formerly one of New York City's finest seafood chefs, had done a complete turnabout by opening BLT Steak to rave reviews in a wealthy yet touristy and aggressively unhip midtown neighborhood off Park Avenue. I had served everyday food in a modern way that was now seen as prescient. But now I was practically going off the grid, and to feed mall shoppers, of all people, not sophisticated foodies willing to drive an hour out into the countryside to dine on Kobe burgers topped with locally raised foie gras.

I had worked hard to earn people's respect, but because my next venture would be at a mall and not in some renovated Boston landmark building, I was seen as a chain, no longer a serious food destination. But my burger bar concept was a standout, and I should have been forgiven my move to the mall. I'd be lying if I said that judgment didn't bother me, but it couldn't be farther than the truth. I am a devout food connoisseur; I am also a businesswoman. Why should the two be mutually exclusive?

Regardless, I had to follow my gut, and my gut continued to tell me that the news I was reading in the paper and online was going to translate into people seeking quality food in a casual atmosphere for a moderate budget. And when they did, they would find me waiting for them, offering an elegant, sophisticated venue that allowed them to play with their food and spoil themselves without getting deeper into debt.

Part of me also wanted to challenge the underlying snobbery of the food world. It was almost as if the critics and chefs believed that people out in the suburbs didn't deserve a great meal. But why shouldn't moms be able to get a great cocktail and a fabulous lunch while shopping with the kids in tow? Why couldn't the hunt for a suit or tie, or even a Mac at the Apple store, culminate with an awesome burger and decadent dessert? Until I came along, people's options were limited to the Cheesecake Factory, Friendly's, and California Pizza Kitchen. I have a lot of respect for these establishments but I thought I could deliver a better-quality product for similar value. There was a whole population out there who knew great food when they saw it, they just didn't have access to it on a daily basis. It was a niche that was practically untouched, and I wanted to fill it.

Once I finally rounded up the approximately $2 million I needed, which included a bank loan, my deal with General Growth Properties fell into place quickly. Remembering my father's advice about location, location, location, I was very specific about where I wanted my restaurant to be situated in the mall. P.F. Chang's was opening there, as well, and I thought it would be wise to choose a location near them since they were at the time the fastest-growing national brand.

Anyone heading over to P.F. Chang's would likely see me, too. In addition, I wanted to be in the middle of the mall, right at the juncture where the old, more moderate retailers met the new luxury ones. That way I'd catch traffic from both shopping demographics, catering to the less expensive side of the mall because I was affordable, but also to the more expensive side because I was sophisticated. I also negotiated a promise from GGP that we could open in Faneuil Hall and that they would give us a large improvement allowance. The deal fell apart, but it was probably for the best. Faneuil Hall would have been expensive to run. And finally, GGP gave us an incentive of $75,000 if we opened by September 15, when the new wing of the mall was scheduled to open.

Then the fun part began—designing the restaurant. I wanted the burger bar to be the star. When visiting Joel Robuchon's gorgeous L'Atelier in Paris, I had been struck by the fun and unexpected juxtaposition between the exquisite, delicate food and the playful, albeit fancy counter service atmosphere. The layout felt like glamorous sushi bar meets million-dollar diner, the center of the room dominated by a long bar facing an open kitchen where guests could watch and even talk to the chefs preparing their meals. Upon my visit to the restaurant I sat down and immediately thought, "Wow!" (Robuchon is a master of the "Wow" factor), "This would be perfect for the burger bar."

Carl and I found an artist in New York City who specializes in capturing images between two pieces of glass, and we commissioned her to create a glass countertop. We had originally hoped to carve the curved walls above the booths out of exotic wood, but when that proved too expensive we put enormous, floor-to-ceiling photographic murals of the locations we honored at the burger bar, so that when we seated people we could say, "Would you like to sit in Tokyo, Paris, or Rome?" We built a beautiful open kitchen for the grill menu, modeled after the now-closed Café Gray in the Time Warner Center in Manhattan. A twelve-seat burger bar occupied a little nook featuring our custom-made dual-sided vertical grill, in essence a second kitchen just for burgers. It allowed the patties to be licked on both sides by the flame, a technique that turned out phenomenally good burgers, the best I've ever had. I was so proud of that grill. (Todd and I designed it and patented it and after a year we had to abandon it because no one would service a grill they hadn't built.) Finally, outside, just as we had in Chestnut Hill, we placed a sign that read, "The MET Bar."

At five o'clock in the evening on September 7 (and $75,000 in incentive money richer, thanks to my deal with GGP), we opened. My father was there, beaming like a very proud Papa Jack among a group of his invited friends. I was so happy to see him. He was ailing, but he was there. He had fought long and hard against his heart condition, getting a pacemaker, pushing himself on the treadmill, and pursuing life as fully and with as much purpose as his weakened body would allow. Part of the way he gained his strength was by immersing himself in his daughters' lives and staying as involved in our business pursuits as we would allow him. Every day, he found his way to Stephanie's on Newbury by lunchtime and the Metropolitan Club for dinner. He wanted so much to pass on his wisdom and to protect us from the same mistakes he had made.

He always had an opinion, which he shared with me whether I welcomed it or not. He had become obsessed by the idea of serving pickled beet salad on the plate as an accompaniment to the burgers at the burger bar. I'd get voice mails from him several times a day, all of them starting the same way: "Kathy, this is your father," as if I needed him to tell me who it was, "I am looking for you." The reasons for the calls varied: to find out the weekend numbers; to bust my chops about the slow service a friend of his had received; to talk about the Sox games; to ask if I knew where my mother was, or when Stephi was due back in town; or to just share with me what he was thinking. It didn't really matter to me why he called. What mattered was that after all those years of trying to get his attention, he was looking for me. More importantly, I had finally earned his approval.

This knowledge is what sustained me when, over the last months of his life, our roles reversed and I reluctantly became an authority figure over him. Parenting children is a rough job; parenting one's parents is excruciating. When he'd rage at me for taking away his car keys or hiring nurses against his will, I'd remind him of what a strict disciplinarian he had been and would joke that he should have thought about how I might take my revenge one day if I ever had the chance. In reality, all I wanted was to protect him from himself and keep him safe; I suppose he had the same intention when he grounded me for a month after catching me climbing out of a third-story window to meet my boyfriend up the street. He rebelled against my restrictions and rules the same way I had against his. He told me I had him in a penthouse prison. I told him that at least the view was good. His frustration was real, but I knew that there was love behind his words, and I believe that he knew the same was true of me.

To the very end, food gave him the will to live. Even during his last days at Massachusetts General Hospital, he had a voracious appetite, wolfing down vanilla pudding sweetened with frozen strawberries with as much relish as if his mother had prepared it. The disappointment in his eyes if I came to visit without a corn muffin stashed in my bag was enough to send me hurtling back down to the ground floor in search of pastry.

There is no way to know whether he was aware that my sister and I held him when he died barely a month after we had opened MET Bar & Grill, on a chilly October morning—the morphine might not have allowed him much of a window into reality. At the very end, when he was set adrift, he seemed to be sailing on some invisible sea. His death was not anything like I feared. It was peaceful. His breathing was shallow, then faint, and then he just followed the roll of the ocean and slipped away.

My grief was overwhelming, but even as I mourned, the business forced me to attention. I had planned to open Natick with one of our managers from Chestnut Hill, Beau Sturm, as GM. Beau was a rock star but it turned out that the mall concept and lifestyle did not appeal to him or his wife, Trina. Two weeks in, around the time of my father's death, Beau gave his notice. I was reeling. My GM gave his notice, my dad was dead, and I had built a beast of a restaurant that seated more than a thousand people on a busy Saturday. I had to build a team quickly. I couldn't do this alone.

I asked my old GM in Chestnut Hill, Mark Peterson, to come work in Natick and apply the same brand of perfectionism there that he had at MET Club. I hired a COO, Jamie Kaye, who had worked for Stephanie five years before and was like a brother to me. Jamie had broken into the business working for The Hard Rock Café back when Peter Morton was still hands-on, and for Pino Luongo at Barney's when the food shop was still downstairs, and I knew he'd teach me a great deal. Jamie can be ruthless. He would kill you over a penny (lucky for us). He is tough but honest with vendors, and he can source anything for the best price. Once he was haggling over the phone and I signaled to him that he'd gone far enough, and he covered the phone and whispered, "Do you want to drive the Mercedes, or do you want this guy to drive it? You can make him richer or us richer, you choose." Point taken.

I also transitioned Jennifer Tradd, who had once done the

marketing and PR for Capital Grille and who had been working for us part time, into handling all of the internal marketing
and PR. Jenn has a very facile, clever mind. She is the go-to
girl in the company, keeping the internal operations func-
tioning like clockwork—menu updates, promotions, emails,
signage. There is little that happens in the company without
Jenn's golden touch. Without this team in place, MET Bar &
Grill would have had a much harder road to profitability and
success.

Yet even with Mark's and Jamie's and Jennifer's expertise
and dedication, getting the new restaurant off the ground was
a battle. Overall, the response from the public was overwhelm-
ingly enthusiastic, but the reality of what it takes to serve six
hundred made-to-order burgers a day proved a greater challenge than any of us had anticipated when outlining the business on paper. I had originally thought I was channeling Ray
Kroc when I conceived of MET Bar & Grill, delivering an
upscale, modern-day version of "what you want is what you
get" to the masses. But actually, my vision was more in line
with that of Starbucks' Howard Schultz. Kroc made hamburgers simple; Schultz made coffee complicated, which is exactly
what I was doing to burgers with my massive, customizable
menus. Both entrepreneurs, however, created streamlined systems that would maximize volume and minimize errors. My
system was still a work in progress.

One bump in particular would teach me a hard lesson. It
was the one time I didn't do things my way, and I got bit-
ten in the ass for it. When I first started MET Club my chef,
Jeff Fournier, and my general manager, Mark Peterson, recommended that I use an employment agency they had worked
with in previous restaurants and that had done business with
big well-known restaurant companies. It was hard to find
people to work in the back of the house, such as busboys

and dishwashers, in Chestnut Hill because though it's on the T Line, Boston's subway system, it's not close enough to the city to be considered an easy commute. Most of these people were holding down two jobs and needed to be able to get from one to the next quickly.

Something about the operation didn't feel right to me. The employment agency would provide us with labor, and we would send them a list of the employees we had used and the hours they had worked. They would send us a bill, and we would send them a check to cover the checks they used to pay their employees. Sometimes the employment agency's checks bounced, and I couldn't figure out why. I was sending them money with which to pay the staff, how could the checks bounce? And why the complicated set up, anyway? It would have been so much simpler for them to pay the labor and for me to pay them back. The whole thing made me uncomfortable, but when I double-checked with my attorneys they confirmed that the system was legal, and I trusted Jeff and Mark, who had worked in restaurants for years and assured me this was often the way things were done. So we hired the employment company for Chestnut Hill and then later in Natick. The arrangement saved us a lot of paperwork, and we were never short staffed. The people they found for us were for the most part earnest and hardworking, and for a while it looked like my suspicions were unfounded.

Then all of a sudden everyone's checks bounced, and we found out that the guy running the company had absconded with about two weeks of payroll. When the Department of Labor stepped in to investigate, we discovered that all along the owner hadn't been paying anyone overtime, either. A law on the books says if you are co-employers, you are equally responsible for any unpaid funds. All along my lawyers had assured me that the people working in my kitchen were the agency's employees, not mine, and that it wasn't my responsibility to ensure that the staff was being paid overtime. But my attorneys were not labor law specialists, and they were wrong. In fact, the employment agency and I were technically co-employers, and when they fled town they left me holding the bag. I was on the hook for about $300,000 for three years' worth of overtime, plus a penalty fee. Of course I wanted to do right by the laborers who had been shafted of their overtime and whose checks had bounced, but it was a heavy price for me to pay. Luckily, I was in a position to absorb the cost of one of the worst decisions I ever made. Lesson learned. From then on I would be adamant about following my gut whenever my team and I disagreed. The other lesson I learned is that when the easy solution doesn't feel right, come up with a harder one and go with that instead.

Operating MET Club and operating MET Bar & Grill were completely different experiences. At MET Club I knew more than half the people on the reservation list. Giving personalized attention wasn't that difficult when you had babysat someone's kids or been to their spouse's retirement party. At the mall, though, a large majority of our guests were walk-ins. Our biggest challenge was to recreate the same personal experience my friends and neighbors received at MET Club for strangers who might just be passing through.

Another difference was how much time I could devote to the restaurant. Since 2004 I had practically lived at MET Club, greeting people at the host stand, having a solid presence in the dining room, hiring, firing, reading the reservations books, and keeping a close eye on all the costs. It just wasn't possible to spend the same amount of time at either location now. My regulars at the MET Club were deeply concerned that I would no longer be a fixed presence at Chestnut Hill. Would it go downhill? I hadn't counted on this particular dilemma. Once your business starts to grow, you need to appear to be everywhere at once. And it takes a lot of work to make sure that you don't start to feel corporate and lose the heart and integrity you had when you first went into business.

And finally, with all my creative and beautiful design at the Natick location, I had created a major conundrum for our kitchen and waitstaff with two separate kitchens—the open kitchen and the burger grill–and one main dining room. In addition, with two entrances, one to the mall and one to the street, I had to staff two host stands. I had built a nightmare labor equation. Over time we fine-tuned our training and communication so that our guests could still enjoy their food the way they wanted it and our kitchen was no longer on the verge of mutiny.

As I grow my restaurants, I recognize how vital training is. It has to be implemented from the day someone walks through the door to work for you. When your business is young it's relatively easy to train because it's hands-on, and you're imparting your own vision and values. But once you get bigger, you have to gather a team that you can trust to transmit that vision and those values as convincingly and thoroughly as you would. Hillstone Restaurant Group excels at training their people, as does Danny Meyer. No matter which of Danny's restaurants you walk into, you are guaranteed the same gracious service. It's a challenge to achieve consistency when you transition from managing forty employees to two hundred overnight. But that's also the excitement inherent in the business—figuring out how to master the challenge and seeing your solutions work. Again, making smart, careful hires made all the difference to our success. I'm convinced that one of the differentiators between our competitors and us is the quality of our product and of our staff.

The first days following a restaurant's opening are the time when you should be making the most money, but it's also the hardest time to do so because you still haven't figured out the rhythm of a place, and the team is still getting to know each other, and you're guessing how many covers and how much labor you'll need, and what your guests are going to eat most—it takes a while to get it under control. I simply had to wrap my arms around the operations. But after just a few months in business, I had no doubt that the concept of MET Bar & Grill had found its audience and would be a popular draw at the mall. Once again, I had ignored the restaurant establishment's naysayers and created my own recipe for success.

My sister said Dad's death gave her a more even keel and made her aware of who she wanted to be as a mother, a wife, and a sister. I reacted with less introspection. I had always worked hard, but now, at fifty years of age, I shifted into racing gear.

Nine

―――――

Balancing Art and Commerce

MET Bar & Grill opened in September 2007, and within a year the housing bubble had burst, Lehman Brothers had filed for bankruptcy, Bernie Madoff was arrested, and the economy was in free fall. People who had invested in the fine-dining echelons of the restaurant world lost a lot of money as patrons turned skittish, snapped their wallets shut, and started eating out more infrequently and more casually. Over time, countless restaurants, especially those with fancy pedigrees, closed their doors. When people did choose to spend their money on a great night out, my restaurants offered a fabulous experience for a reasonable price, so we absorbed displaced patrons seeking new options.

My business plan had factored in a weakened economy and people's increasing penchant for casual yet innovative, exciting food, and we were well situated not only to survive the downturn but also to quickly turn a profit despite the country's bleak financial outlook. By focusing so heavily on profitability, we could increase the value of our backers' investments, but also buy ourselves the time we needed to build the company without having to take on excessive risk. Still, we weren't unscathed. Sales did drop, and consequently the bank took the opportunity to accuse us of not meeting the covenant of our loan, and calling it in. Our agreement was contingent on my company grossing a certain amount and netting a certain amount, and we weren't doing either. Sales dropped considerably, our food costs went up, and labor costs remained high. I had no choice but to pay the loan back using my inheritance from my father.

The sinking economy was terrible for all retailers, including those at the mall in Natick. It had been positioned as a fancy shopping destination. The owners had made a grave error by not seeing the signs that the economy was heading south, and they had populated the entire new wing of their mall with stores like Neiman Marcus, Chanel, and Louis Vuitton. Everything in that part of the mall suffered enormously. Because of my location in the middle of the mall, however, I held my own. I was special enough for those shoppers who weren't terribly affected by the economy, and affordable enough for those who had to watch their wallets a little more closely. Paradoxically, it was the poor economy that opened the way for me to grow my business faster than even I had planned.

A new lifestyle mall called Legacy Place was being built in Dedham, about twenty miles southeast of Natick. It had a lot going for it that we'd had in Natick—close enough to grow the brand, not too close to the other restaurants to cannibalize them, plenty of floor space, outdoor seating, and foot traffic—but it was not anchored by a big box store like a Neiman Marcus or a Nordstrom. There was an L.L.Bean and a Whole Foods, but Chase Chavin had advised me to be wary of places anchored by grocery stores, even high-end ones, because they don't drive business. People shopping for food aren't thinking about going out to eat. In addition, the spaces available didn't sing to me. Yard House was opening up right across the way, and I saw them as direct competition at lower price points. All and all, I was not that interested. WS Development, the owner of the mall, was persistent, however, and I had to turn them down several times.

Then something interesting happened. Ruth's Chris Steak House was supposed to open in Legacy in a space located directly under P.F. Chang's, but when the economy tanked they pulled out. Around the same time, I came to the conclusion that Neiman Marcus wasn't driving any business to MET Bar & Grill in Natick. Any success we were having had nothing to do with being located near an anchor store. In fact, we were doing well in spite of the mall, which was simply too luxury-oriented. They had concentrated all of their high-end retailers on one end, without even throwing in a Starbucks as a lure for people whose original destination might have been the less-expensive side of the mall.

So, knowing that the MET Bar & Grill concept didn't need a high-end retail anchor store to succeed, when Ruth's Chris pulled out of Dedham and left a space open directly under a P.F. Chang's of all places, I saw kismet at work. I told WS Development, sharpen your pencils if you want to make a deal. That was an old phrase of my dad's. It meant to a negotiating partner, come back to me when you've got some numbers that will work better for me.

If you can master the art of the deal, you will ensure that you can earn a living in the worst of times and thrive in the best of times. The trick, as my father explained to me, is always covering your downside. That means that when you calculate your proformas—your hypothetical revenue based on past experience and operating expenses—you cut them in half, and then approach the negotiating table. That way, whatever you agree to, you won't overstretch your budget. And if you perform as well or better than you did before, you'll be that much ahead of the game. By the time the deal was done, we had negotiated an extremely favorable deal. We took over the space in 2009 and opened our second MET Bar & Grill.

A part of me was nervous about opening another restaurant so soon after the first MET Bar & Grill, but I remembered the advice my mother drilled into me: you have to spend money to make money. It's not possible to grow without putting in capital and taking some risk. She was so progressive for her time. Part of what held my father back when he attempted to open his own restaurants was that he had a hard time following that advice. He was a man who lived in the present, and it pained him to spend money on anything that didn't offer immediate returns. My father may have been the entrepreneur, but it's possible that my mother's business instincts were even sharper than his. She was better at projecting into the future and calculating how expenditures today would pay off down the road. That probably explains why, years after they divorced, my mother had positioned herself into a far stronger financial situation than my father. Every time we'd talk about my business she would say emphatically, "Kathy, you have to invest in your future and yourself." So that's what I did. Carl and I didn't go back to our investors to ask for money, we put our own money into the company.

I was spurred on not only by personal ambition but also as a way of coping with the loss of my father. Three restaurants in five years—he would have been proud. And in those five years I learned something important, which is that while growing a successful business is a matter of balancing risk and reward, most of all it's a matter of trusting your instincts and listening to people. My father excelled at the former but refused to do the latter. I, on the other hand, do both, listening to everybody, synthesizing what I hear, and then doing exactly what my gut tells me to. I was told that the suburbs were a dead zone for innovative food. I was advised that no shopping mall could deliver the demographic I hoped to attract. I was warned that people would be confused by the concept of a burger bar. Over and over again people had questioned my calculated risks, and over and over again I had proven that if there was one thing I understood, it was what people wanted when they were deciding to eat out. It made me wish that I could go back in time and reassure my parents as they tore their hair out over my expulsion from prep school that their daughter's maverick tendencies and affinity for risk would actually help her survive in life.

We navigated some bumps. In Dedham, parking proved to be a real issue. Even though retail employees were supposed to park in employee parking, they often parked in the customer spaces. The mall offered valet parking, which mitigated that problem for those willing to pay, but then they reduced the valet hours, which meant that in order to shop at Dedham, shoppers had to traverse a parking lot the length of a football field. People wearing expensive shoes aren't going to do that.

But by far the worst occurrence was when I learned that on Super Bowl Sunday two young women had had drinks at MET Bar & Grill in Natick, gone upstairs to another restaurant to continue their revelry, and then, after leaving the mall, crashed their car into a family driving home from a ski trip. We agreed that we bore some responsibility, and had our liquor license suspended for one day. I lost sleep for months fretting over the realization that decisions made at my restaurants could have far-reaching implications long after our guests had left the restaurant. We had always had a strict policy about not selling shots, about to whom we served alcohol, and about how much, but after that we became even more vigilant. We fired the waiter who had served the girls and made everyone go through another round of alcohol training. I did everything I could to impress upon my staff that, when in doubt about a guest's level of intoxication, they were to refuse service, and I would back them up every time. There was simply no other way to handle the situation. While we never confronted circumstances like that again, the diversity and the transient nature of our Natick and Dedham clientele offer a unique challenge to my entire staff.

Aside from these unfortunate instances, the majority of my dilemmas took the form of compromises that I wished I didn't have to make. The double-sided grill that I had been so proud of in Natick turned out to be a money pit, unable to handle the volume of our restaurants and requiring constant service. When we opened our second location in Dedham, we didn't install another vertical grill and we closed off the kitchen from view. I hated to sacrifice the beauty and drama of the open bar, but there were just too many days when the kitchen was in a frenzy trying to keep up with the flood of customized demands of our guests, and I didn't think the public needed to see how much work and sweat went into turning out their meals. Like anything else in the entertainment world—a dance performance, a play, a movie, even Disneyland—getting the full experience relies on the audience giving itself up to a little bit of magic. With a closed kitchen, we could preserve the illusion that our guests' meals were prepared almost effortlessly.

At Metropolitan Club I'd always handed guests two menus—a regular menu and a bar menu when they sat down. At first I did the same at MET Bar & Grill, offering guests a bar-and-grill menu and a burger bar menu. It quickly became clear that our guests were suffering from information overload. Eventually we combined the menus, placing the burger menu at the center and surrounded it with the offerings from the bar and the grill. We wound up increasing the number of burgers sold, which I would have thought impossible because we already sold so many. At this point, at least 60 percent of our sales are burgers. Highlighting them allowed us to focus the brand. It was the kind of discovery you make only after you've had time to look at and listen to your business for a while, to figure out not only who you are but who your guests think you are. It took years for Stephi to identify herself as sophisticated comfort food. You have to be clear about your brand from the start, but you have to let your customers help define you as well.

There were small disappointments. Todd and I concocted a burger bread that I was sure would be a huge hit. We baked meat and cheese into a loaf, and it tasted like a baked cheese-burger. It was amazing. Who wouldn't want one? Just about everybody, as it turns out. Nobody would buy it, and we couldn't figure out why. The best reason we could come up with was that maybe people wanted to eat burgers, and adding burger bread to the mix felt like overkill.

MET Bar & Grill Hamburger Bread

Yields: 4 loaves

Focaccia dough (see recipe)
4 to 4 ½ cups grated cheddar/ mozzarella mix
1 batch hamburger filling (see recipe)
¼ cup extra virgin olive oil
¼ cup raw sesame seeds
All purpose flour for dusting work surface
Egg wash
3 cups Parmesan cheese for dusting crust

1. Dust work surface with flour.
2. Divide the focaccia dough into 4 balls.
3. Roll each into a rectangle still leaving the dough thick.
4. Splash the extra virgin olive oil in the center, spread around with hand.
5. Heavily sprinkle cheddar /mozzarella mix. Spread evenly over dough.
6. Spread ½ cup (3 ½ ounces) of hamburger filling over the dough.
7. Sprinkle cheddar/ mozzarella to lightly cover hamburger filling.
8. Roll up in a pinwheel (be careful not to stretch dough), seam should be on the bottom.

9. Spray with egg wash to cover all showing sides.
10. Sprinkle sesame seeds on top.
11. Sprinkle parmesan cheese on top.
12. Chill for 1 hour.
13. Repeat steps 3 more times.
14. Cook on parchment- lined sheet pans for 15-17 minutes at 350 degrees, convection, high fan.
15. Cool to room temperature.
16. Blast freeze.

Focaccia Dough

    4 teaspoons yeast
    2 cups warm water (110°)
    1½ cups extra virgin olive oil
    4 tablespoons sugar
    16 cups all purpose flour
    2 tablespoons salt

In a mixing bowl, combine yeast and warm water. Add sugar. Stir to dissolve. Add flour and salt. Add oil. When the dough starts to come together turn mixer up. Mix dough until forms into a ball. Add more flour if it is too sticky. Sprinkle counter lightly with four. Place dough on counter top and lightly knead. Place dough in oiled bowl, covered and let rise for an hour. Roll out according to directions above.

Hamburger bread filling
Yields: 4 loaves

    2½ pounds ground beef
    2 each red onion, small dice
    5 Roma tomatoes seeded and small diced
    6 ounces smoked bacon chopped fine
    3 ounces unsalted butter, chilled and small diced

¼ cup oil blend
Salt and pepper to taste

1. Preheat a heavy-bottom rondo pan.
2. Salt and pepper the ground beef.
3. Hard sear ground beef in oil.
4. Cook beef to medium rare.
5. Turn heat off.
6. Add diced red onion and tomato.
7. Mix well, adjust seasoning.
8. Cook bacon crisp.
9. Mix with hamburger mixture.
10. Cool, add chilled butter.
11. Mix well.

———————

Then the burgers, and the system we used to assemble them, had to get makeovers. It was taking too long for guests to get their orders, so we had to change the fat content in the meat so that the patties would cook faster. In a completely contradictory move, however, I also forced the line to adopt a slower method for assembling the burgers. Originally, we decided that as the line read the incoming tickets, they would lay the toppings on the bun and then drop the burger on top. But though the technique made for fast assembly, it also made for a ridiculous-looking burger. I asked the line to find another efficient way to assemble them. They ended up building from the top of the bun first, not the bottom, and then flipping it right side up before taking it out to the guest. It made the burgers harder to build, but they looked much better, and we were still able get them out within a reasonable amount of time. As my mother taught me many years ago, presentation matters.

Figuring out reliable systems that would allow us to

balance the needs of our guests—like fast turnaround—while still maintaining our strictest standards of quality proved to be a constant challenge. Setting high expectations is a double-edged sword, particularly for the MET Bar & Grill restaurants. If I had designed the spaces to look ordinary, or even like a diner, guests would have been thrilled out of their minds to get the kind of food and service they received. Though people hope for the best when they go into a diner, most of the time, you get what you pay for. At MET Bar & Grill, however, the price isn't driving the expectations; the basic burger only costs around nine bucks. The environment, however, feels four-star. The result is that sometimes people hold us up to the standards of an actual four-star restaurant. This is my constant conundrum: How do I continue to exceed people's expectations, offer stellar service, and still provide value? I want to serve on beautiful Staub dishes and use delicious Marcona almonds, but will those choices drive the business enough to justify the cost? If Staub dishes and Marcona almonds are that important to me, how many burgers do I have to sell to pay for them?

As our COO Jamie Kaye always loves to remind me, you can't pass the costs on to the guest. We offer a lot for free, like the onions, tomatoes, and lettuce on your burger, charging only for the specialty toppings like blue cheese or guacamole. This is as it should be, but we still have to pay for those onions, tomatoes, and lettuce somehow. I want to create art, but I want to make money doing it. How much will people pay for a customized burger? These calculations have to be part of your business plan from the start. Restaurants are a nickel and dime business, but you can't let people feel like they're being nickel and dimed. On the other hand, no one ever made money giving his art away for free.

When I moved into the malls, some people in the restaurant world probably disdainfully accused me of sacrificing art for commerce. Aside from the fact that the quality and presentation of the food I serve in my restaurants is very good, there is an art to providing the kind of quality at the volume that I do. Consistency in and of itself is an art, requiring a fine-tuned coordination that is only possible with smart hires and superb training. Restaurants thrive when people trust that they will receive the same great food and service today that they did the last time they came to dine with you. Nobu Matsuhisa, one of the most brilliant chefs of our generation, understands this well. It doesn't matter if you're downstairs in the Aspen restaurant or in the one on Fifty-Seventh Street in New York, the food and service are consistently exceptional. Though he has opened restaurants in sixteen cities, no one dismisses Matsuhisa's business for being a chain, if they even recognize it as such.

Consistency is the key to doing well, and it's a four-star son of a bitch, as my father would say. That's why it's so important that your sous chef, your GM, your chef, and all the people at the front of the house, in the back of the house, and up and down the line and the chain of command, understand your vision. It's relatively easy to control the consistency of your food and presentation when you're only seating sixty people per day and have a total of fifteen items you have to prepare. When you've got hundreds of covers, plus a huge menu that changes seasonally, plus the reputation for willingly accommodating people's whims and preferences, you've got a potential catastrophe on your hands if your systems aren't tight. When you're slammed, it's easy for your priorities to change from delivering a beautiful product to just getting the dish the hell out of the kitchen. To avoid that situation you have to stay on top of every detail, because details do matter.

The following sign, in English and in Spanish, hangs in all five of my restaurant kitchens:

WHEN I MET FOOD

MET CARDINAL KITCHEN RULES

French fries: HOT and CRISPY
Hard-boiled eggs: EIGHT minutes with a soft center
Omelettes: French style—FLUFFY and crisp on outside, soft
    center inside
Greens: NOTHING brown—throw it out!
Lobster roll/salads: Meat is cut in CHUNKS—NOT minced
Hamburgers: TEMP and perfectly cooked to proper temperature

> NO Precooking
> NO Squishing
> TOAST & BUTTER all buns

Steak: All temped TO ORDER; NO end/vein pieces
Sandwiches: All spreads and ingredients are COAST TO COAST

When the tuna tartare is usually molded into a perfect square, the guest is going to be taken aback if it arrives on her plate round. It's a jolt, a minor one, but one that in a subliminal way can affect a diner's experience during her meal. You've got to make sure that you deliver what the customer expects. If the menu says that the sandwich is served on Tuscan wheat bread, it's got to be served on Tuscan wheat bread. And if you don't have Tuscan wheat bread, don't put it on another kind of bread, because the guest who has come in and ordered the sandwich is going to be let down if he gets a different sandwich than the one he thought he was ordering. Go to the supermarket as fast as you can and get what you're missing, or don't serve the sandwich. The customer may be disappointed, but at least now you have the chance to wow him with another menu option.

People don't like change. Unless you've branded yourself as a place where the menu rotates constantly, people's emotional connection to their food can make it tricky when you want to make changes to your menu. For example, I figured out that I can't play too much with my bar menu. We came up with a dish we called steak snacks, which was like an egg roll stuffed with steak, onions, and cheesy mashed potatoes. People loved them, but they complained—loudly—when they weren't perfect, which was often. In an attempt to improve the product's quality and consistency, we tweaked the recipe, filling it with less meat, cheese, and peppers. Again, people complained, this time because their beloved steak snacks had changed into something more akin to mashed potato snacks. We couldn't get the product right, so we took them off the menu. And people complained. We were damned no matter what we did. It got to the point where I wished I'd never introduced steak snacks in the first place (although when they were good, they were very, very good). We got so much grief for taking our mozzarella sticks off the menu (for the same consistency issues as the steak snacks) that we're putting them back on.

Crispy Steak Bomb Snacks

Serves 8 to 10

> 2 pounds beef sirloin (fat removed and thinly sliced)
> 2 poblano peppers (thinly sliced)
> 1 white onion (thinly sliced)
> ⅓ cup white cheddar cheese (shredded)
> ⅓ cup block mozzarella cheese (shredded)
> ⅓ cup Comté or Swiss cheese (shredded)
> 2 baked Idaho potato (diced)
> 12 spring roll wrappers
> Olive oil
> ½ liter corn oil or vegetable oil for frying

Water
Salt and pepper

1. Boil Idaho potatoes. When soft, place through a ricer into a bowl. Cover and reserve.
2. Sauté onions and peppers together in olive oil. Cook 10 minutes or until soft. Remove and place in bowl.
3. Reheat pan and add olive oil, then add seasoned beef, cook for 6 minutes or until meat is medium-rare.
4. In a large bowl mix beef, peppers, onions, cheese and riced potatoes.
5. Add salt and pepper, then cool.
6. Lay one sheet at a time of the spring roll wrapper out in front of you so that the square looks like a diamond with one of the tips pointing at you.
7. Place a tablespoon and a half of the filling in the center of the wrapper. Brush water around the wrapper. Then fold the tip over the filling, roll upwards once, then fold the sides into the center, roll upwards again. Brush a small amount of water on the tip and on the rolled log where the tip will meet and press when the two meet. Place on wax paper.
8. Repeat 11 more times.
9. Heat fry oil to 350 degrees (if you do not have a home fryer then please use a candy thermometer).
10. Fry two to three at a time for 3 to 4 minutes or until golden brown. Serve hot.

Two Dipping Sauces

Steak sauce mayonnaise

1. Mix 2 cups mayonnaise with 1 cup of your favorite store brand steak sauces.

Wasabi Mayo

1. Mix 2 cups mayo with ¼ cup of wasabi paste. Then add ⅓ cup simple syrup.

———————

Every restaurateur is forced to compromise between art and commerce every single day. For example, charcoal is hands down the best heat source for a burger, but if I used charcoal my guests would have to wait three times as long to get their food. Chefs, too, make compromises like that every day in their kitchens—at least, those who want to make any money. That's the big difference between running a restaurant and running a restaurant business. You have to be willing to make sacrifices when you're growing a restaurant business, not just because of the financial consequences when your expenses outstrip your earnings, but because an unwillingness to compromise can get in the way of acknowledging and delivering what the guest wants.

Business is an art, but chefs are actual artists, and I think sometimes that artistry can be hard to manage. In other eras, guests were content with being told what to eat and how to eat it, but today people are accustomed to feeling like their opinions and preferences matter. Whether or not that's a good thing is beside the point. It's just a fact, and anyone hoping to open a restaurant to showcase her art has to factor that very commercial reality in to her decision making. You need to let people express their genius. If you're a really good restaurateur, you find a way for the artist to have an outlet to create, and you find a way to do it in a financially responsible way. Sometimes that means making the kinds of decisions that can be difficult for an artist to swallow.

Delivering what the audience wants has been my focus throughout my career, whether I was working in film or in food. Case in point, the biggest blowout Bob Richardson and I ever had centered on an art versus commerce showdown. We were shooting a commercial, really more of a public service announcement, for Rainforest Crunch, which was going to funnel proceeds for the candy to an organization dedicated to helping indigenous populations. We were on a limited budget, and spent ten days in the Costa Rican rainforest filming. We were close to getting all the footage we needed when Bob decided that he didn't like the way the commercial was scripted to end. He felt that if Rainforest Crunch really wanted to save indigenous cultures from extermination, we had to dramatize in graphic detail what would happen if people didn't support the cause. His suggestion was significantly more violent and would cost more money than what the client had asked us to deliver.

I understood Bob's feelings, but I thought what he wanted to do was over the top. I had promised the client that they would get the commercial they asked for, within the limits of their budget, and that was what they were going to get. Bob and I went head to head over the issue, and in the end I prevailed. It may have been the first time I ever stood my ground against Bob, and he didn't expect it. Nor did he speak to me for a long time afterward. Bob is a true artist, and what he wanted to do for the commercial would probably have been brilliant and provocative. But as much as I would have loved to see his creativity unleashed, my responsibility financially was to the client.

And now my responsibility is to my guests. I'm not interested in serving anything other than outstanding food, which can be a tough standard to live up to when you've got as many people coming through the door as I do. The battle is to build and maintain a big business while keeping my initial heart and integrity, so my ego is wrapped up in providing the best food and atmosphere possible for my patrons. Aside from that, it's really my guests, and not necessarily my personal preference (although the two often align), that determines the way my restaurants are run. When they wanted classic food with a twist, I gave it to them. When they wanted more bar seating, I gave that to them, too.

Granted, sometimes I had to figure out what they wanted before they even knew it themselves, in the vein of Steve Jobs, who famously said, "It's not the consumers' job to know what they want." That's how we ended up with televisions in all of my restaurants. Mark Peterson, my general manager when I opened MET Club, was horrified by my idea to put TVs in the bar area. Few if any steak houses had TVs at the time. Mark came from a traditional background and believed that people went to bars to connect with each other, not glue their eyes to a television screen. They could do that at home. But I insisted. We lived in one of the most sports crazy towns in the country, and I knew that if given the option, people wanted to see the games. Mark and I dueled over this issue for weeks, but I won, and now our bars are packed every day with people talking, laughing, and happily keeping an eye on the score. For the record, Capital Grille now has televisions in every restaurant.

Giving people what they want is just good business, so that's what I try to do. Someone with a bigger ego might have resented the idea that a game, and not the food or the ambiance or the aroma, could be the major draw that brings some people to her restaurant, but I know better. Food is sometimes the last reason people go to a restaurant, and I have no problem with that. I simply make sure that anyone who comes to me because I happen to be airing the right game walks out of the restaurant raving happily about his meal, even if he is also raving like a madman about the unfairness of the calls. I spend my life caught between the precarious lines of art and commerce.

The debate between art and commerce is inherent in

every decision a chef or restaurateur makes, from how much truffle oil to add to the Indian corn with toasted fregola, to how many people to hire, to the brand of window cleaner to use. It's a decision between art and commerce every time you have to figure out what incidental items you'll offer for free and which ones cost extra. If you want your guests to experience something fabulous, such as wagyu beef or caviar, unless you're comfortable charging an arm and a leg, you first have to figure out how to offer a small amount that still feels generous. For someone like me who spurns moderation, making such a decision is agonizing. For example, we serve hazelnuts with our crispy Brussels sprouts appetizers. They are Trufflebert Farm's hazelnuts from Oregon—they're the size of acorns, very special and pricey, the best you can get, and their flavor is amazing. I'd love for the whole plate to be covered with them, but we finally had to limit the kitchen to exactly ten hazelnuts per dish, because otherwise we were losing money with every order. We could have solved the problem by going with a more common type of hazelnut, but I would have been miserable every time I watched a plate of Brussels sprouts come out of the kitchen decked in ordinary hazelnuts when I knew there were better ones that would elevate the dish to a whole new level and make my guests swoon. Art versus commerce—you make your money in between the cracks.

MET Back Bay Brussel Sprouts, Hazelnuts, and Pecorino

Serves 4

> 3 pounds Brussel sprouts
> ¼ cup olive oil
> 1 teaspoon Maldon Salt

½ pound slab bacon, cut into thick lardon ½ inch x 1 inch
4 ounces shaved Pecorino cheese
Handful toasted hazelnuts, roughly chopped

Preheat oven to 400 degrees. Peel outer leaves of Brussels sprouts and trim. In a sauté pan cook the bacon. Once crisp, set aside. In the bacon oil mixed with ¼ cup oil, sear Brussels sprouts over a high heat until crisp on outside. Continue roasting in oven until fork tender. In a bowl, combine with lardon and cover with shaved Pecorino and chopped hazelnuts. Salt to taste.

———————

Three restaurants in five years is a lot to juggle. What made it even more challenging is that the whole time I was opening the third restaurant, in Dedham, I was also in the midst of building my fourth restaurant. MET Bar & Grill in Dedham was a fluke, a total testament to the art of the deal. Before I ever signed the Dedham lease, I had already decided that I was ready to work on something different from the slightly off-the-beaten-path venues I had chosen for MET Club and the first MET Bar & Grill. When a once-in-a-lifetime opportunity arose to open a restaurant on one of the most desirable and popular streets in Boston, I had to take it. But the decision presented the biggest dilemma of my life. I would open my fourth restaurant, but in the process I would lose my sister.

Ten

—————

The Hardest Decision

They say that you don't really grow up until your parents die. But there was a period in between opening the Natick and Dedham MET Burger Bar and Grill locations when I reverted a bit to my younger self, rebuffing the sadness that threatened to swallow me whole after my father's death by immersing myself in work but also by playing harder than I had in years. In the face of death, I felt urgently compelled to live life to the fullest, and I craved more connection with the people I loved and went out of my way to spend as much time with them as I could.

Ali had moved to New York City shortly after graduating from Brown to pursue a career in film, and Bob Richardson was also there shooting. My mom had a wonderful apartment in the city where I could stay, so I would go as often as possible. Bob had just lost his mother as well, so together in the spirit of celebrating life we ate and drank with abandon, indulging in sublime sushi and a mind-blowing bottle of Chateau Y'quem at Masa and pink Champagne and caviar at Caviateria. I flew back and forth from Boston to LA to see every one of my twenty-year-old son's theatrical performances at USC, and while there splurged on white truffles and Sassaccia at Giorgio Baldi and Japanese wagyu and an expensive bottle of Staglin at CUT. Then back to New York, where I'd party and dance until four in the morning at the 1 Oak with my twenty-three-year-old daughter. I shut the bar down with old friends at the Box. I was out of control, and I liked it. It was during this time, shortly after opening in Natick, that my mother hosted an engagement party in Palm Beach for my niece Courtney. I flew in eager to celebrate the beginning of a new happy chapter for our family.

As I've said, I don't believe opportunity knocks; it doesn't make things easy by grabbing your attention. Rather, I think opportunity is the door itself, open and waiting, and it's up to you to be aware enough to see it and walk through before it closes. Over my career I've been good at spotting these doors and, being the adventurous type, gamely stepping through. And yet, I almost skipped right past one of the biggest opportunities of my life, not because I didn't see it—truly, I would have had to be blind to miss it—but because I wasn't sure I wanted to face the consequences of taking it.

My mother had invited a close friend to the party, a well-known lawyer who had handled a number of restaurant deals. I was just popping a crab puff into my mouth when he sidled over to tell me that he had visited my restaurant in Natick and loved the whole concept. Then he added, "I know about an opportunity on Newbury. How you do you feel about that?"

For twenty years the space in question had been the location of well-loved restaurants—Joseph's during the '60s and '70s, and then Joe's American Bar and Grill. The lease was coming up, and Charlie Sarkus, Joe's owner, whom my dad had financed, had decided not to renew his lease and to instead move to a new location up the block. The landlords wanted to secure a new tenant before Joe's moved out. They had eaten at Chestnut Hill and loved the food and the concept, and thought I might be the right person to take over the space. And what a space—a gorgeous historic 1887 townhouse on the corner of Dartmouth and Newbury, in the heart of the posh Back Bay neighborhood, filled with luxury retailers and art galleries. The only problem was that it was also one block away from Stephanie's on Newbury, the gem of a restaurant Stephi had transformed from struggling food shop to bustling Boston institution. How did I feel about that? I replied to Larry, "I'll never say never, but that could be problematic."

Stephi and I had been the very best of friends. Our DNA ran deep, but we spent time together because we wanted to, not because we had to. We traveled together, vacationed together, skied together, raised babies together, and cooked brilliantly together. We shared an unspoken language and saw much of the world the same way. Very few sisters have that connection. There was no one that I loved more.

She was a little fancy; I was a bit more laid back. She was calm and single-minded; I liked to have ten different pots boiling on the stove. I could make her laugh like nobody's business, but she had the uncanny ability to make me—and indeed anyone—feel like the most important person in the room. My sister's pain was my pain. And I believe for many years that feeling was reciprocated. When Stephi met the man who would become her second husband and I met Carl, our attention naturally shifted. But things really began to change between us when I opened MET Club.

All our adult lives we had supported each other in our respective careers. I had always been proud to admit that, yes, Boston's beloved answer to Paula Deen (though Stephi is a lot cuter) and the Queen of Patio Dining, as she had become known in the press, was my sister, and she had always been supportive of my endeavors in the film world. She had extended me a lifeline when my marriage fell apart, allowing me to work in her kitchen while I licked my wounds and reconfigured my life. She was generous.

But she had taken it hard when I decided to make a go at

a career in restaurants. Before, we had each been ruler of our own domain, but now I was moving into her territory, potentially poaching an identity that she had worked hard to establish as her own. She's naturally competitive, but she didn't want to be put in a position to compete with me, or be compared to me. Her concern wasn't entirely misplaced, either. As I assured her would be the case, we don't compete. In fact we probably strengthen each other's identity. But it is true that as soon as MET Club opened people did start comparing us, often favorably, but sometimes not. To make matters worse, her version of how I landed the Chestnut Hill deal and my version were quite different.

My father had approached Stephanie a good year before I signed the lease to ask if she was interested in the space vacated by Todd English. He told me that she had pointed out the severe shortage in parking and said she would never open there. So as far as I knew, she had turned the space down. But according to Stephi, she had never definitively decided against the idea, so she was shocked when she called me to tell me she was considering opening in Chestnut Hill and before she could get the words out I said, "Guess what? I'm doing Chestnut Hill!" I thought I was taking something she had rejected, and she thought I was taking something that wasn't rightfully mine. Now I can see why she would be upset, but there was no way I could have known that at the time.

It was many years after opening in Chestnut Hill that I would learn Stephi's version of the story. I felt sick. Seeing the situation from her perspective wouldn't have changed my decision to open a restaurant—even when I was working in film I knew that one day I would want to get into the food business, and if I hadn't started in Chestnut Hill I would have simply started elsewhere—but it would certainly have helped me understand the depth of her resentment and maybe given us a way to begin talking though our feelings. Years later we would ask ourselves, did Dad pit his daughters against each other on purpose? I doubt it. The more likely explanation is that my father was a man who lived in the moment, and at that moment the only thing he was concerned about was finding someone to pay the debt Todd English owed him. He knew he could get one of us to do it. I suspect he never considered how such an arrangement could affect his daughters' relationship. But sadly it did, and I was so excited by the attention he paid me once I had become part of a world he loved and understood that perhaps I didn't recognize how deeply Stephi's feelings were hurt. That said, I believe she was happy that my dad was paying attention to me.

Stephi struggled to contain her feelings for a long time. She attended the MET Club opening, admiring what we'd done and saying only that she hoped I knew what I was getting myself into, because she feared I was still romanticizing the business. She knew how tough it could be, how the pressure and the schedule and the scrutiny from the public and press could wear on you. You really have to be built for the business to enjoy it, and no one, including myself, knew what I was made of yet.

In the years following the MET Club opening I proved that I was indeed cut from the same cloth as my dad and Stephi, but as often happens when cracks in the relationships between family members and loved ones aren't immediately repaired, distance set in, and the silence between my sister and me continued to deepen as I received more press and expanded my brand. It was only in the few months before her daughter's engagement party that we had started reaching out to each other again. Progress was slow, but we were finally beginning to heal the rift between us.

But now this. I had successfully brought metropolitan dining to the Chestnut Hill suburb and to the Natick mall, but I had yet to try introducing the Met concept to the actual metropolis. To firmly establish my brand in Boston proper, I knew that I needed a key location in the city, and suddenly I had one in the palm of my hand. I had to at least take the meeting. It was with the knowledge that I could undo all the progress we had made and lose my sister forever that I hesitantly agreed to meet with the landlords. They were impressed with what I had done with MET Club and MET Bar & Grill and thought I would fit in well in Back Bay.

Before I walked into the Back Bay space I had been thinking that if I were to go forward—and given the strain I suspected it would put on my relationship with my sister, it was a big if—it might be a good place to open a second MET Bar & Grill. That idea changed as soon as I walked through the door. Many restaurateurs develop their concept long before they ever take over a physical location and adjust the space to fit their vision. But I've always let the space speak to me and inspire my concept. Perhaps I was subliminally influenced by the Capital Grille situated just up the street from Metropolitan Club, but when I walked into the Chestnut Hill location it seemed to scream, "Steak house!" As I walked through the mall location I couldn't shake the feeling that it was begging to be something more beautiful and exciting than your typical mall offering. Here in the Back Bay, the space was regal. On the outside, 279 Dartmouth Street was a gorgeous, four-story red brick and brownstone townhouse. Inside, beneath the dated and worn Joe's eighties-style interior, I could see the bones of a classy grande dame who wanted to be treated with a little refinement. My imagination started firing. With its multiple levels and nooks and corners, this place could be the epitome of the concept I had introduced when I highlighted the MET Bar within Metropolitan Club and the burger bar within MET Bar & Grill—it offered the chance for many different experiences under one roof.

Though the building was landmarked, and beautiful, it would need a significant facelift to bring it up to date. Therefore, the landlords were willing to offer us a twenty-five year lease. No one gets twenty-five year leases, much less in an historic, upscale, heavily trafficked shopping district. I feared that I was sitting in front of a once-in-a-lifetime opportunity.

I walked away telling the landlords that I would have to give the offer some serious thought, and then I proceeded to stall for as long as possible, secretly hoping that the issue would somehow go away and the decision would be made for me. They were patient, for a while only checking in with the occasional friendly e-mail, but by July they had no choice but to step up the pressure for an answer. I couldn't avoid making my decision any longer. I had to go talk to my sister.

I drove to the Cape to meet her near her summerhouse at our once-favorite spot in Cataumet called the Chart Room. I started out anxious and defensive and probably mishandled the whole conversation right from the beginning, as one usually does when one fears the outcome. After hiding behind some small talk, I finally said, "I have an opportunity, and before I tell you what it is..." She interrupted me. "Is it this?" No. "Is it that?" No. I finally blurted out, "I have an opportunity on Newbury Street." Although I immediately followed up with all the reasons why I felt I had to go forward, I don't think she heard much after "Newbury Street."

I hoped I could mediate the situation by suggesting that we open the restaurant together, but she wasn't interested. I should have known. For a while she did a food show on TV, and I, with my extensive production experience, had suggested that maybe I could be involved. She was very clear. She said, "Kathy, business is business, family is family, and the two should never meet." She had set a precedent.

She had built her business and her brand all on her own, and had never had to consult with anyone else when she was ready to move in a chosen direction. She didn't want to have to concern herself with anyone's vision or opinions but her own. She also had no interest in going into business with family. She was convinced such an arrangement would end in disaster, which hurt my feelings, since I'm always so optimistic. I would have jumped at the chance to partner with her. I tried my best to convince her but she wouldn't budge. In retrospect, she was probably 1,000 percent right. When we were children, Stephi was a champion ice skater—she's always been a lone artist. If she's on a team, such as the one that makes a restaurant run, she's managing it, not playing for it. I'm a leader but I'm also a team player. We would have likely clashed.

Regardless, I was tortured by the decision I had to make. I loved no one more than my sister, and I could see the pain I would cause her by opening a restaurant less than a block away from hers. But ultimately it came down to survival. This opportunity could be an important step in growing the business that was going to pay my bills, fund my retirement, allow me to be generous with my children and their future families, and return my investors' money.

I tried to explain why I didn't think my move would have the negative consequences she predicted. Her brand was already thoroughly entrenched in Boston's psyche; no one was going to confuse her sophisticated comfort food with my modern concept. I didn't believe that I would siphon away her business, either. From my experience in the Natick mall, I knew that having a cluster of good restaurants in close proximity to each other was actually great for driving business. Nor was I establishing a brand-new competitive presence on her street: there had always been an American restaurant on the site I was taking. I wasn't taking anything away from her or introducing any kind of threat. But it was about the principle. All she could see was that now, instead of just encroaching on her territory figuratively, her little sister was encroaching on it literally.

In every way I could, I tried to get her to understand why I had to accept the opportunity before me, but her feelings of betrayal persisted, and so did the tension between us. After a lifetime of closeness, the distance was excruciating for both of us. The whole debacle began with a conversation at Stephi's daughter's engagement party, and from then on we saw each other only at these kinds of formal family functions that we were obliged to attend, such as her daughter's wedding, my wedding, and our father's unveiling.

The situation saddened my mother terribly, but when I asked her whether she thought I had overstepped my bounds, once again she showed me that behind that beautiful and perfect ladylike exterior hid a heart and mind that could have belonged to any of Boston's toughest business moguls: "You earned this opportunity," she told me. "You take it. Don't let anything get in your way."

I signed my new lease in Back Bay in October 2008, about twelve months after opening in Dedham, which had made money from day one and was providing the cash we needed to open this new concept. We immediately started renovating, capitalizing on the Victorian-era penchant for cozy spaces, alcoves, and big windows. Looking over the blueprints with my architect, I saw a small room right in the middle of the second floor, just above the stairs. I imagined that once upon a time it might have been a private library lined with floor-to-ceiling shelves of books, a quiet space where a person could lose a few hours curled up with a novel and a snifter of brandy. And so it became The Library Bar, where we serve crafted cocktails with hand-chipped ice. The small room is lined with banquettes and tables along two walls, and is dominated by a softly lit mirrored bar where I interspersed some lovely vases and old books pilfered from my mother's house, in between the bottles of liquor.

Off to the side, Joe's main dining room was transformed into the sunny Living Room, an open, clubby space from which guests could look out on a panoramic view of the busy street through the long wall of seven-foot-high windows. Downstairs, at street level, became the MET Bar. I split the counter in two. On the left stood a twenty-four-seat traditional bar serving every libation you could want. On the right was a ten-seat ham and cheese bar, where guests could drink while watching their bartenders expertly cut slices of artisanal American-made prosciutto and other cured meats as well as domestic cheeses. I split the bar in two for practical reasons—I needed to create a pathway from the kitchen out to the Terrace, our outdoor dining space—but aesthetically it provided yet another way of making every visit a unique experience depending on where guests sat. The wall on one end of the room was covered with a blackboard where we listed all the specials, and we installed a small, sleekly modern fireplace at the other end.

Joe's had been equipped with two kitchens, one located down in the basement, and one on the first floor leading out to the bar. I thought it would be easier to expedite and supervise all of the food if it came out of the same place, and decided to use the first-floor kitchen. That left an empty area, which became Townhouse. It's a dark, sexy room lined with mini chandeliers, banquettes, and intimate two-tops. With its deep red walls, on which we had a local artist scrawl T.S. Eliot's poem *The Love Song of J. Alfred Prufrock* in black, and sketches of glamorous old-time movie stars like a young, pouty Liz Taylor, the feel is a bit bordello. Adding to the mystery and sense of exclusivity, guests enter through a private, unmarked door. Walking into Townhouse is like being welcomed into a secret, exclusive club. Unlike New York City and LA, conservative Boston may not appear to have the kind of nightlife that would support a private lounge, but the more people found out about it, the more calls we got about hosting private parties.

My goal was to create a beautiful restaurant that would appeal to any mood and any occasion. You could have lunch with your mother in the sedate library one afternoon and return that night to rock it out at the loud, crazy bar downstairs. The only thing that would be the same no matter where you sat was the great food.

I put a little bit of everything I loved on the menu, capitalizing on the broad spectrum of tastes and styles available to me thanks to the cosmopolitanism of the MET brand: scrambled eggs served any time of day; a grilled artichoke inspired by a gorgeous dish I had at Club 55 in Saint-Tropez; Allen Brothers' steak; Dan Tana's chicken Parmesan; a balsamic brick chicken from Primola in NYC, served on the bone; all of our top-selling burgers from the burger bar; and all of the favorites like the tartare duo from MET Club. In an ode to our predecessor, Joseph's, we did a take on their fantastic shrimp curry, upgrading it and making it our own with basmati rice, dates, toasted cashews, and coconut. We also introduced what would become our top-selling dish, a micro-chopped salad, truly the king of its kind. Tiny, perfectly cut pieces of beets, red onion, avocado, broccoli, eggs—anything you could imagine—were all tossed together into a riotous mound of color and texture and fabulousness. It would become so popular I'd have to put it on the menu at MET Club in Chestnut Hill. We also do a handful of small salads at the MET Back Bay, both hot and cold. This is one of our top sellers.

MET Back Bay Truffle Indian Corn and Toasted Fregola

Serves 6, as a side dish

- 2 cups cooked fregola (follow directions on package and slightly undercook)
- 2 cups creamy corn (recipe below)
- 3 teaspoons truffle peelings
- 2 teaspoons white truffle oil

Heat in sauce pan and cover with ½ cup Parmagiano Reggiano cheese. Broil until brown.

Creamy Corn

12 fresh ears of corn
3 minced shallots
1 cup heavy cream
2 tablespoons butter
1 tablespoon chopped, fresh thyme

Shuck corn, scrape kernels and milk from cob. Melt butter, sweat shallots and thyme together. Add corn. Add cream. Add corn cob for flavor. Reduce by half. Remove corn cob. Puree half of your remaining corn and cream mixture in a blender. Add puree back to creamed corn and reduce again by one quarter. Cool.

And finally, when guests sitting at the ham and cheese bar were handed their wooden boards heavily layered with charcuterie and cheese, they'd find it dressed with perfect accompaniments like quince, Marcona almonds, and sweet dates.

Not everyone got the idea of a ham and cheese bar. My team really questioned my judgment on that one. Ham and cheese? *Locally made* ham and cheese? That's it? They were thinking too narrowly, not realizing that there had been an explosion of small artisan charcutiers, dairy farmers, and cheese mongers who were introducing unbelievable American-made pork products and cheeses that were beginning to rival anything found in Europe. I loved the idea of giving people a little altar at which to worship such a simple, satisfying combination as ham and cheese. It also continued a MET theme that people were coming to expect: a surprise concept inside every restaurant. Each restaurant had a little jewel hidden inside it—the bar menu at MET Club, the burger bar in the MET Bar & Grill, the ham and cheese bar, and in my fifth restaurant, MET on Main in Nantucket, a tartare bar. I feel like each one is a little gift, a special spot in my what-you-want-is-what-you-get restaurants where guests get one more opportunity to mix and match to their hearts' delight. Outside MET Back Bay, as I had in all three of my other restaurants, I placed a sign announcing the MET Bar. By now I didn't really have a choice—the MET Bar had become my core brand. People expected a great bar—one that offered something special—wherever they saw the MET name.

That branding element of providing unique bar experiences has become one of the main draws to our restaurants, but it has introduced its own challenges, too. It doesn't happen as much anymore, but in our early days we'd get people at Chestnut Hill who had dined in Natick and wondered why at Chestnut Hill we only offered select combinations of the continental and international burgers that appeared on the Natick menu. People would go to Natick and be disappointed that there was no ham and cheese bar. As our brand grows there is less confusion, as more people know who we are and what to expect of their experience with us. We've transcended our name, much like Cheesecake Factory, where everyone now knows you can find a hundred menu options besides cheesecake, or California Pizza Kitchen, which serves pizzas, of course, but is also well known for its salads and small dishes. We are rarely called MET Club or MET Bar & Grill anymore. Now we're more often referred to as MET Chestnut Hill, MET Natick, MET Dedham, and MET Back Bay. Becoming bigger than your name should be one of the primary goals for anyone hoping to grow a big business. It's a sign that your customers have absorbed and embraced the essence of your brand.

That lovely, brand-enhancing ham and cheese bar was a contentious topic at my house for a while. The renovations for MET Back Bay were a huge undertaking. Carl and I get along famously except when we're building a restaurant together. Inevitably, my practical, responsible husband and partner sets a prudent, reasonable budget, and I immediately get to work blowing it. I can't help it; I want everything to be the best.

Carl and I went head to head over the expense of renovating MET Back Bay. For example, he almost had an aneurism when he saw the price of the gorgeous white marble I chose for the countertop of the ham and cheese bar. I could have selected something cheaper, like a Carrara with its distinctive grey veining, and it would have looked great. But I don't like the gray veins in Carrara marble. I wanted the bar to have that pure white glow you find in sculptures. "You think anyone is going to notice the gray veins?" he said to me in that frustrated tone he uses when he thinks I'm being unreasonable. Of course not. Guests would have noticed the marble, not what kind. But I would have noticed, and it would have forever bothered me that the bar didn't look as beautiful as it could have. Carl was 100 percent right, and I completely disregarded his advice. Any other choice but my expensive, milky white marble would have looked ordinary, and I can't do ordinary. I didn't go into business to do ordinary or average. How would I be serving my guests if that were the best I could aim for? Where's the pride and victory in that? It's true that plenty of restaurateurs, and entrepreneurs in general, have ruined themselves by refusing to adjust their dreams in the face of certain market or budgetary realities, yet no successful restaurateur or entrepreneur has ever built anything memorable or lasting by settling, either. We're always in a tug-of-war between art and commerce, and there is no rule that can tell you when you're making a good investment, and when you're making a foolish one. Deciding what will drive your business and what is worth an extra expense is terribly subjective. Carl and I are constantly at odds with each other over this. I'll want to put out lanterns and flowers in the garden, and he'll tell me that some nice tables and chairs will look just fine. But I want to make magic, and sometimes that takes money. On the other hand, spending money on magic usually means making compromises elsewhere. You just have to figure out where your compromise will be least noticed.

On October 25, 2010, almost three years to the day after my dad died, MET Back Bay opened its doors. The night was stunning, a quintessential Boston fall evening. Bathed in the warm glow of sconces and fireplaces, humming with laughter and conversation as people enjoyed their food and drink, the restaurant felt enchanted. At the end of the night, after almost everyone had tripped out into the chilly night, I sat in Townhouse and wept. Opening any restaurant is stressful, but the two years leading up to this moment had been especially draining, emotionally and financially. The undertaking was hugely expensive, imposing a tremendous financial risk on my young business that I wasn't sure I could recover from if things didn't go as planned. But as soon as the doors opened, I knew my judgment had been sound. (In fact, not only would MET Back Bay be profitable from day one, but also MET Bar & Grill in Dedham would pay itself off in an absurdly short amount of time.) Yet while my tears were of joy and relief, they were also tears of grief—for my father, who could not be there to see what I had accomplished, and for my sister, who I feared might never come to my restaurant. Some business decisions we make over the course of a career are almost not worth the price of success.

Stephanie's Chase-Away-the-Blues Biscotti

Makes 32 biscotti

1 cup whole almonds toasted
1 cup pecans toasted
2 cups of chocolate chips
2 Snickers bars, chopped
1 stick softened butter
1 orange rind, grated
1 ½ cups sugar
3 eggs
4 ½ cups flour
2 teaspoons baking powder
1 tablespoon good quality vanilla
½ teaspoon kosher salt

Beat butter and sugar until soft. Add eggs, orange rind and vanilla. Beat until well blended. Add flour, baking powder and salt slowly to the batter. Do not over beat. By hand, add both nuts, chocolate chips, and chopped Snickers. Mix until well incorporated. Shape the dough into 2 logs and place on a cookie sheet. Bake in a preheated oven at 325 degrees for approximately 40 minutes or until golden brown. Take out and turn oven down to 200 degrees. Let logs cool. On a diagonal cut logs into ½-inch-thick cookies. Place on a cookie sheet and bake at 200 degrees for 1 hour or until the cookies are crisp and golden brown.

Eleven

Tweeting Truth to Power

One month after opening MET Back Bay, a column appeared in *Boston Globe* Magazine naming MET Club one of the top ten influences on Boston's evolving dining landscape. The piece called us a "Tastemaker," and the author, Devra First, applauded my "one-step-ahead modus operandi." I was appreciative. It wasn't the first time someone had identified my efforts in similar terms, but it was the first time I'd seen it in print. I was thrilled that she got what I was trying to do. To my knowledge, I did a burger bar before anyone else in Boston, and a ham and cheese bar before anyone (and by the time this book comes out I'll have done the first tartare bar, too). It felt validating to have my vision and my work publicly acknowledged. To finally be seen.

Three months later, in February, First reviewed MET Back Bay. Sadly, you can't bat 1000 all the time. The title of the review was strong, "MET Meets the City," with a subtitle announcing, "Back Bay eatery could become a hot spot." The review itself read well and felt worthy of three stars yet it resulted in only two (out of four), but the criticism was fair and she expressed optimism that we could shore up our weaknesses. Most of her negative comments, as well as those we were getting from our guests, centered on the fact that the service was not what they'd come to expect from a MET restaurant. The three-level building and multiple-room layout was making it hard for managers to keep an eye on everything and fix problems before guests became aware of them. Most of the quibbles about the food were also indirectly caused by the logistics of getting our timing right and handling the myriad custom orders from our large menu. As usual, we spent our opening months working out all the kinks, and as a result of that review I invested in a new, more rigorous training program to help eradicate the service issues that kept cropping up.

Waiting for that first review for MET Back Bay was a far less nerve-wracking experience than when I'd opened Chestnut Hill five years earlier. At that time I couldn't think about anything else. I felt exposed. I had a lot at stake given my family history, and since everyone knew me in the neighborhood there would be nowhere to hide if the review was poor. When the first review for Metropolitan Club finally came out I was in Israel with my daughter. We were on a bus on the way to Haifa when I checked my e-mails and saw that my guys had forwarded me the review from the *Boston Globe*. The reviewer, Allison Arnett, wrote that our foie gras appetizer was "as simple as a little black cocktail dress and as elegant."

I loved that. Classic and refined, just what I was after. She called Jeff Fournier's version of a chopped salad, "outstanding." She raved about the desserts. And still we only got two and a half stars. I was disappointed. Based on her compliments, I thought we deserved three. The chopped salad we started out with at Chestnut Hill was deservedly praiseworthy and popular, but over the years we've enhanced it even more and now it's consistently one of our top sellers.

The Ultimate Chopped Salad

Serves 2

> 4 ounces chopped romaine lettuce
> 2 ounces chopped broccoli florets
> 2 ounces diced red onion
> 2 ounces chopped hard -boiled egg
> 1 ounce chopped bacon
> 2 ounces diced beets
> 2 ounces diced tomatoes
> 2 ounces fresh corn
> 2 ounces shredded cheddar cheese

Toss with Italian dressing (recipe follows) and top with ½ avocado.

Italian Dressing

> 1 cup red wine vinegar
> 2 medium shallots, chopped
> 1 tablespoon Dijon mustard
> 1 tablespoon salt
> 2 teaspoons black pepper
> 2 cups canola oil

Combine first five ingredients and stir well. Add oil, whisking constantly to emulsify. Pour over chopped salad.

I was frustrated when I looked closely and realized that her main complaint was simply that we were yet another steak house, no matter that we had pushed the boundaries of classic steak house cuisine. In other words, I was penalized for my blockbuster format, the exact reason I wanted to open the restaurant in the first place.

It galled me that MET Club didn't get a higher rating—when you're used to getting As, and you've worked hard to earn one, a B can feel like a failure. And I chafed in general at the ratings system because it allows no way to qualify the stars one receives. To whom were we being compared? Were we two and a half stars compared to Noma, to Capital Grille, or to Outback Steakhouse? That detail would make a huge difference, and there was no way for the public or us to know. Apparently, however, Arnett's words of praise resounded louder than the rating she gave the restaurant, because business at MET Club boomed from the day the review came out, and after that positive word of mouth kept the momentum going.

By the time I opened MET Back Bay, five years after my first restaurant, I was less nervous about reviews and felt confident and secure that I was making good decisions all around. MET Club had consistently made it to most of our area's "Best of" lists and the burger bars had received enthusiastic thumbs-ups, and thus I felt a tad more impervious to criticism. A less-than-perfect critique like the one we'd received from the *Boston Globe* wasn't the end of the world. We were well on our way to building a brand that resonated way beyond one review. Chestnut Hill is a sleepy suburb and the Metropolitan Club there is a destination restaurant, so it was far more dependent on the press and word of mouth for its survival. The location in Back Bay afforded us a luxury that is uniquely different, with foot traffic, and lots of it.

However, nothing could have prepared me for the shock I felt when I read the next big review from one of the city's major publications. Corby Kummer's opening line read, "MET Back Bay serves factory food in a factory setting." Ouch. The opener was painful but the real problem was a few lines down. I had known Corby since we were both freshly out of college. He had gone to Yale with my ex-husband and we had many friends in common. In fact, I had had dinner at Corby's home several times. If only I could have published a review. Those meals had always made me question how Corby landed a job reviewing food. Perhaps I sound bitter, but it's important when reading or receiving reviews that you keep in mind who is writing them, so that you can be discerning about how much credence it deserves.

Corby couldn't help but mention that he knew me through my first husband, to whom I hadn't been married in fourteen years, and that they went to college together. What relevance did any of this have in the review? He'd never mentioned this fact in any previous article. The review was harsh; it was personal, and therefore, vitriolic. It sounded as if Corby resented the fact that a large-scale operation had opened up in the Back Bay and had the promise to make money. I had read his reviews over the years and detected a bias toward small restaurants, the ones in bombed-out locations run by couples with a baby in a bassinet tucked away behind the kitchen, eking out a living on a shoestring budget serving thirty covers a night.

I was spitting mad, but not because the review was negative. Had it been a fair evaluation, the criticism would have stung but I would have compared it with other feedback I'd received and used it to help me decide if we needed to make some changes. I had read the first review and had appreciated that the reviewer saw not only the glitches but also the potential. This one was mean-spirited, condemning the place because he thought it was designed to make money. He walked through my doors determined to dislike the restaurant. In fact, I was present both times he dined with us. From what my staff and I could see, he barely ate.

He tried to soften the blow of his damaging words by admitting that the restaurant's concept did in fact work, and he praised the one thing that the kitchen didn't cook, the ham and cheese board. Brutal. Once again, I was being accused of sacrificing art for commerce, when in fact I had simply enthusiastically embraced both.

Had this review come out in 2004, it may have had an impact on MET Back Bay. But 2011 was not the same world. Once Twitter came on the scene in 2007, everything about the way people learned and talked about the restaurants in their cities and towns changed. By now the impact of a review in any of Boston's major publications was significantly diminished by the rise of social media and peer review sites like Yelp, Open Table, City-search, and UrbanSpoon. Reviewers simply didn't have the clout they used to; they were just one voice among a thousand others.

Professional critics can prime the pump, but in reality, it's always word of mouth that is going to determine whether the public embraces or rejects a restaurant. The power of social media existed long before the computer. People have always trusted their friends more than anyone else to tell them the best places to eat—the Internet has simply made that word of mouth fly faster and go farther. Social media has been a godsend to anyone with a business, allowing owners to extend their brand and find avenues to people's hearts and minds that they never would have had access to before. It allows you as foodista, restaurateur, or guest to be part of an ongoing dialogue, a bigger conversation, an interactive cyber world in which we can rave, rant, and share our opinions on subjects we are passionate about, such as food. As a restaurateur, you can learn a lot about how the public sees you, and, best of all, respond.

I love Twitter, and I consider my posts there, my Facebook page updates, and my blog, *Kate's Dish*, all ways to reveal the person behind the brand. (My best friend Jayne started calling me Kate while we were in college, and I've always preferred that nickname to "Kathy." It's the one my closest friends use.) Social media offers a window into my life. Anyone following can get a sense of how I live, what I eat, the places I frequent. It gives life to my voice. I love how social media allows us to give our customers a peek behind the curtain. We live in a voyeuristic world where reality TV reigns supreme, and I guess you could say social media is an extension of that, to some degree. People want to know more and more about each other—why not about the personalities behind the businesses they love?

My strategy is simply to post what's authentic to me and to take the opportunity to talk about what we're offering to the public, whether it's the burger of the month, a new watermelon yuzu martini, or the announcement that we're opening up a fifth restaurant.

Last year, my team—Todd, Jamie, Stephen, Jenn, and I— taped a six-minute segment, called "24 Hours with Kate," for a local television station, which of course we also posted on our YouTube channel. The show chronicled the research trips we take together a few times a year, eating our way through our favorite shops and restaurants in our favorite cities. I thought it would be fun to capture our three-day eating adventures and condense them into twenty-four hours, during which our fans could see where we get our inspiration. It was a video travel guide, highlighting the best places to eat, sleep, and shop. It was my first time in front of the camera for any appreciable time, and so I relinquished my producing hat.

We had a blast and it was a terrific bonding experience for my team, but I found it frustrating because I wasn't in control of the footage. The producers only wanted to reveal the positive angles, which means that the world never knew about the places we went where we weren't impressed. The outtakes would have proven way more gritty and interesting than the complimentary clips that were chosen to air. I was frustrated that some of the funniest and most interesting moments happened off camera, like when we were traveling home from Portland stuffing our faces with pie, sharing stories about previous trips we'd taken or disastrous meals we'd eaten. It was hard being on the other side of the camera for the first time but it was a lot of fun, and I saw it as yet one more way for me to share the things that give me pleasure with the rest of the world.

For the most part, there are two kinds of online reviewers, the haters and the fans, and unfortunately, people who have a bad experience are far more motivated to have their say. That explains why if you go on most social media or peer review sites, you will find many more negative reviews than positive ones. In restaurants as in life, the sad truth is that people are extremely likely to tell you what you've done wrong; they're slower to tell you what you've done right. (That's something I think about constantly when I'm talking to my staff. I am strict and demanding, but I make a conscious effort to let people know when I see them doing great work.) Some negative online comments don't mean that the restaurant isn't great; they mean that the majority of people who had a great experience just haven't bothered to voice their opinions online.

Restaurateurs and other retailers who expose themselves to public opinion have to toughen up, but no matter how seasoned you are it can still hurt to read negative comments. It doesn't matter how many successes you have behind you, opening a restaurant is no less stressful and terrifying for an owner than opening night of a play or the premiere of a movie is for the actors. No one can fathom the amount of sweat and work it has taken you to birth this baby. Online reviewers don't think about the consequences of their words, and they can be cruel and callous. But you have to listen, even when you'd rather not. You have to figure out a way to get to the truth, to determine who has a legitimate complaint and who just likes to make noise.

I'm grateful when people take the time to share their experience with me. I want to know the truth. I spend a tremendous amount of time online evaluating what is being said about my restaurants. When I hear something positive, nothing is more satisfying. And when I don't, I try to learn from the experience. We still provide comment cards at every restaurant, and I read every single one of them. I read every letter that comes in and we're aggressive about responding. We are constantly engaged in dialogue with our customers. I tweet and post constantly, and if I'm not doing it my son Ben is. We'll talk ahead of time to set up exactly what he's going to tweet about which restaurant, and when, and then we'll create a schedule through HootSuite. He's constantly checking in with me to make sure that he's getting my voice right, and checking in with Jenn Tradd to make sure that we're hitting all the right notes at the right time. In my eagerness to share information, I tend to get excited about things, and he gets annoyed because I'll tweet about something we've already agreed he was going to post himself. But whether he's typing in the tweet or I am, the message is always coming from me. We try to be selective about what we post. In the course of a day there are thousands of things we could tweet about, and we want to be careful that we don't over saturate people with too much MET. Twitter is the quick hit, what we use to capture the here and now. We send out e-mail blasts to announce events, big menu changes, or birth announcements for a new restaurant. Facebook is also a quick resource for people to see what's going on currently, but it's also like a permanent photo album or diary that people can review any time they like. Social media is a perfect way for people to get to know me, and for me to stay abreast of how they feel about my business. For the most part people love us, but when they don't, I want to know about it.

Ben responds to every negative comment, and we do what we can to make things right if someone has had a poor experience. If someone gives us fewer than three stars we invite him back, on the house. We know that if we hear the same negative feedback more than once, it's not just one cranky person complaining, it's a real issue that needs to be addressed. Often the comments and e-mails we get simply reinforce a problem I have already brought up to my team and am working to solve. Social media has put power into the public's hands, and it has been a gift, albeit an odd one, to restaurateurs who genuinely care what people think. And yet, when I really want to get a sense of how well we're doing, I still do things the old-fashioned way. I sit in the restaurant and watch.

On any given day you can usually find me at the front of the house, often plunked in the middle of a busy banquette, trying to look inconspicuous as I monitor people's body language and listen for any hint that will tell me more about how my guests experience the restaurant. What impression do we make as they are escorted to their table? What happens to their eyes as they take their first look at the menu? Do they smile when their food arrives? Has their conversation died down because they are happily enjoying their food, or is something wrong? This is where and when you get unadulterated honesty, not from a critic, not from an online "friend," but from watching your guests' faces as they eat your food and interact with their surroundings. Sites like Yelp are fantastic tools; they act as extra sets of eyes. Yet I don't trust anyone's eyes as much as I trust my own.

Fortunately, most of the time I like what I see. Nothing makes me happier than seeing people eating, laughing, and having a good time. If there is any message I want to convey— whether it's through social media, a fabulous meal, or even a book—it's that there will always be a beating heart and a progressive mind behind my business and all of my restaurants.

Twelve

Coming 'Round Full Circle

I step off the ferry and the world recedes. For me, arriving on the island of Nantucket is like going back in time, not just because of its history or the old windmill and pre-Civil War buildings, or because it is such a timeless place—a fairy-tale setting where captains' homes and cottages line cobblestoned streets and locals do business with a nod and a handshake—but also because I feel a deep connection to the place. It evokes so many special memories from my past.

Here I was a girl on a boat, sailing with my father every Fourth of July weekend, unpacking the lunch I had prepared so carefully to please him. Here I was a young woman working my first summer job doling out cream-and-coffee fudge ice cream so I could be nearer to the boy I loved. Here I was a mother who watched her son become a man in a beautiful bar mitzvah ceremony under a round tent at dusk with our closest friends on the beach the weekend after 9/11, the sky overhead a pristine blue unmarred by flight trails. Here I became a wife when Carl and I married in an untraditional ceremony where our kids acted as the officiants, and the chef, who had once worked for my sister, created the most incredible sashimi, crudo, and sushi spread I have ever had. Here Carl and I raised our children; it's the place where we have spent every August and Labor Day eating freshly harpooned swordfish or just-picked heirloom tomatoes and corn from Barlett's Farm, or my homemade midnight turtle cookies.

Kathy's Midnight Turtle Cookies

32 large cookies

1 pound butter, room temperature
2 cups dark brown sugar, packed
3 ½ cups all purpose flour
1 teaspoon sea salt
7 ounces bittersweet chocolate, shaved
2 cups toasted pecans, chopped
¾ cup chunky peanut butter
12 ounces Rolos candy, chopped

1. Cream the butter and sugar until light in color.
2. With mixer on low speed, add the flour and salt and mix until the dough begins to come together.
3. Add remaining ingredients, mixing just until dough forms a ball.
4. Roll the dough out onto a floured surface to 3/8 inch thickness.
5. Cut the cookies out and place on parchment-lined cookie sheet.
6. Bake at 325 degrees for 10 to 12 minutes, turning the pan at the halfway point.
7. Cool and store in an airtight container.

This is where we come to reconnect, relax, and replace the sounds of the city with the sounds of chiming bells, buoys, and boats in the harbor. And now, it's the place where we will come to work, to create fresh memories as we open our newest restaurant, MET on Main.

Why Nantucket, when it has the same major drawbacks that kept me from opening a concept in Atlantic City? It's true that the population only swells to about fifty thousand in the summer, and I'll have a short, four-month window in which to make real money before the summer ends and the cold winds start whipping along the beaches. But Nantucket is no ordinary island; it's an internationally renowned destination. Some of the wealthiest people in the country have homes here. Though it is a seasonal place to do business, it has cachet that will enhance my brand in a way that Atlantic City never could. Nantucket evokes the same romance as Gstaad, Aspen, Palm Beach, and Saint-Tropez. It is a special place. A magical place. And in the time since I considered Atlantic City, I came to realize that Chestnut Hill is a bit of a seasonal business itself because all the residents flock to the beaches for the summer. An island restaurant could actually be great for cash flow, acting as a seasonal counterbalance.

In the early weeks of building the restaurant during the off-season, few places were open on the island. Carl and I stumbled into Le Languedoc, a lovely French inn and bistro on Broad Street, and ended up there three nights in a row. Since then we have made it our weekly if not biweekly haunt. Why? Not only is the food very good but the bartender, Jimmy, is phenomenal. He is an excellent reminder of how a great bartender drives business, particularly on this island. We learned quickly that it was essential to get Jimmy's number if you want to scoop a seat at the restaurant's charming ten-seat bar. Luckily, Jimmy complies.

One night, we started talking with the restaurant's gracious owner. We learned that, along with Le Languedoc, he owns a pizza place near the ferry dock called Steamboat Wharf Pizza. I had just signed my lease, and I asked him, "Does anyone make any money here?" His reply: "Let's just say it's more about lifestyle than it is about money." That's not the most encouraging answer this business owner has ever heard. That said, he has been very smart. His French inn and restaurant is his pride and joy, but his wife says she would rather own ten pizza shops than one French restaurant. After 11 P.M., you can only buy Steamboat Wharf Pizza by the slice. At $3.75 a slice, that pizza allows he and his wife a comfortable life and supports their fairy-tale island lifestyle. They are proof that it is possible to balance art and commerce on a small island if you are fastidious about keeping tight control on your food and labor costs to maximize your earnings.

Establishing a presence in Nantucket will certainly help expose us to a national and international crowd, which will hopefully help us further the growth of the MET brand and take us into other viable markets. Though opening a relatively small restaurant on a small island might seem out of character for me, when I have made such a point of going big, there is something to be said for having a varied portfolio. Besides, I've never been one to limit myself to just one thing. It's nice to have the opportunity to do something different, something that's not big, and not in the city, something that's more intimate and personal. I love Boston and I love my other restaurants, but it's possible that this beautiful little signature space in Nantucket may be the one that makes me happiest of all.

I'm excited but also nervous about opening a business in a place where I have such a deep connection. I searched for the right location on the island for two years, and the whole time I wondered, is this even a good idea? Will I be able to make the clearheaded, objective decisions necessary to keep a business profitable when I have such a strong emotional attachment to it? Will I be able to smoothly ramp down the business and the menu from serving seven hundred covers during the summer to serving only seventy during the off-season? My labor pool will be small, so will I be able to hire for the kind of quality and service I'm known for? Am I being willfully blind to the risk because I so deeply want to establish new roots on this island that I love so much?

Only time will tell. After spending so much time hunting for the right property, I finally was able to make a good deal. Everything about the way it came about told me that this was "the one." First, the opportunity arose because the owner of a beloved restaurant called The Even Keel Café, one of Nantucket's few remaining year-round businesses, had decided not to renew his lease, and the landlord found himself in the position of having no tenant or being forced to run the café himself. It had taken me this long to find a place to open because most of the real estate proposals I'd heard from other landlords gave them every advantage and offered me very little in return. This landlord's predicament meant there was a possibility I could negotiate a real estate deal that worked for both of us.

Second, this opportunity was the first that allowed me to mark a number of boxes off my mental checklist. Location? The address is smack in the middle of Main Street on one of the most beautiful islands in the world, so even though we couldn't possibly do the same volume as at my other restaurants, we would be able to capitalize on what foot traffic exists. Outdoor seating? The space has a gorgeous outdoor patio. Year-round appeal? If we remained open for at least eight months out of the year, we could become a place that the locals embrace and call their own. Unlike most businesses on the island, we'd be open early for coffee and breakfast and stay open late for midnight snacking. From what I see and what people tell me, there is a need for our kind of business here.

The landlord and I were equally motivated to make the deal work, and it only took us ten days to come to mutually agreeable terms and sign a lease. Talk about the art of the deal. It's like this was meant to be, and I don't say that lightly. It's the third reason I was sure this location was the right setting for my newest venture. Almost forty years ago, the Even Keel Café was the site of a store called the Sweet Shop, where I held my very first job, the one where I gained a little bit of weight from scraping the sides of the fudge bins after closing time.

There was one final sign that I took to be serendipitous. I was just closing the deal with the landlord while having lunch at the Peninsula with my sister, who had moved to the Los Angeles area about eighteen months earlier. I hung up the phone and she asked, "What was that about?" I hesitated to answer, not sure what she'd say. "I've been looking in Nantucket." She smiled over her fresh fruit and yogurt. She told me that Leo, her right-hand man, had been negotiating on the very same space. My heart sank. The last thing I wanted was to go through this again. She paused for a minute and said, "You know, Kath, you have long loved the island. It makes sense for you. I'll tell Leo to step away." And she did.

Recently, Stephi was in town looking at another space on Newbury Street that might be available, currently occupied by a saloon called Charley's and owned by the same people who own Joe's American Bar and Grill. I told her that they had contacted me to see if I was interested in the space, and she looked at me and said, "We may want to do that." I said, "Go for it." What a difference a year and a half makes.

That Stephi and I can now share lunch and talk shop is a testament to the healing properties of time. It does not necessarily heal all wounds, but it does allow you to gain some perspective and to let your emotions simmer down. There was a long silence between Stephi and I after I opened MET Back Bay, but in time, slowly and carefully, we started trying to repair our relationship. The catalyst was an event that I spearheaded to honor my father, a fundraising benefit for the Massachusetts General Hospital Heart Center that took such good care of him when he was ailing. I couldn't bear the idea of doing it without Stephi. I called her and explained what I wanted to do, and asked her if we could join forces. She said yes. That joint effort gave us the opening we needed to start communicating again. We are one hell of a team. Together we organized a spectacular night of food and drink featuring the talents of everyone who knew and loved my father, those who could point to him as the person who had given them their shot as well as all the people fostered by that generation of chefs. There were so many of them—Todd English and Jasper White, Barbara Lynch and Steve DiFillippo, Tiffani Faison, our own Todd Winer and Jeff Fournier, and on and on. We called the benefit, "How Jack Stirred the Pot." That he did, without a doubt.

It's incredible how life comes around full circle. I can sit on the back balcony outside my bedroom window and look down on the business where I worked when I was eighteen years old. Except now it's mine. But even as the sounds of construction pound through the air and I watch it transform from sleepy little café to sophisticated restaurant and cool island bar, the spirit of everything that has gone before is still there. I think my father would love my new concept. Unlike the Sweet Shop, MET on Main, as the new restaurant will be called, will not necessarily wreak havoc on anyone's diet. Before I knew anything else about the concept, I knew that the menu would have a tropical feel and reflect the island propensity for bikinis, shorts, and flimsy summer dresses. Developing the menu has been a blast. I'm excited about the dishes Todd and I are developing, such as a divine batch of short ribs marinated overnight in Chinese black vinegar, oil, mirin, ginger, soy, and a hunk of brown sugar, then coated in water chestnut powder (it delivers great crunch), deep fried, and topped with hot orange oil. It's to die for. But what to call it? The right name is Brown Sugar Beef. I would eat that in a heartbeat, but a lot of girls wearing bikinis might not. Maybe we don't highlight the sugar. Maybe it's called Hot Orange Beef. Menu wording and placement is an art unto itself.

With the amount of bare skin on display on the island, people are in the mood to eat light. In a departure from my regular meat-centric menus, there will be some burgers and a steak or two (and marinated short ribs for sure), but overall the menu will be a compilation of fresh and light Asian, Polynesian, and Mexican-inspired dishes named The Cabo, The Jamaican, and The Bermuda after other beautiful island destinations. And though it will be unlike anything I've done before, the restaurant wouldn't be a MET without a little have-it-your way surprise inside. One of my top-selling items has always been my tartare duo, and there's no better skinny food, so MET on Main will feature what is to my knowledge the first tartare bar, where guests can choose from a beautiful selection of yellowfin, salmon, and local catches, as well as less traditional choices like beets and other raw shaved vegetables, combined with an array of seasonings and fresh herbs. It's been fun to play with the tartare concept. A great restaurant really is all about the bar, and how high you're willing to raise it. I hope the concept is as well received as my burger bar and American ham and cheese bar.

MET's Original Chestnut Hill Duo of Tartare

Serves 4 to 6 people

Tuna Tartare

    16 ounces #1 sushi grade tuna, handcut into tiny cubes

    2 ounces cilantro

2 tablespoons fresh minced ginger
2 tablespoons finely diced shallots
Spicy mayo*
¾ cup soy sauce
¼ teaspoon Yuzu

*Combine ½ tsp Sriracha chili sauce and ½ cup spicy Kewpie Japanese mayo. If you can't find Kewpie, add a few drops of mirin and rice wine vinegar to Hellmann's which will make it tangy and round it out.

Start with spicy mayo and slowly add in soy sauce and Yuzu until emulsified. Mix into diced tuna and then fold in ginger and cilantro. Season with sea salt.

Salmon Tartare

16 ounces of handcut salmon in tiny cubes
Ponzu Sauce*
2 ounces diced red onion
2 ounces chives, sliced on the bias
Sprigs of micro cilantro
½ quart of orange juice
¼ cup rice wine vinegar
1 cup sugar
¼ teaspoon cornstarch
1 cup of soy sauce

*Combine orange juice, soy sauce, rice wine vinegar, and sugar and reduce by half. Mix corn starch with water to make a slurry. Whisk into reduction and thicken sauce.

Combine spicy mayo with the ponzu and mix into the salmon. Add diced red onion and chives. Season with sea salt. Serve with taro chips or deep fried shrimp chips. Place the duo next to each other on a plate in two different small ring molds about 3 inches round and 2 inches high. Pat each tartare tightly into the mold on the plate and lift mold off the plate. Garnish with micro cilantro and chips of choice.

That said, not long before we began construction I had an epiphany. It followed a conversation with Tiffani Faison, a Top Chef runner-up who worked with Todd English and Todd Winer before working for me in Chestnut Hill for a few months, where we became fast friends. She is crack smart and a terrific sounding board, and I'm always eager to share ideas with her because I know that she will inevitably respond with something provocative and unexpected. She will push me to see things I might not otherwise see. We were having dinner and discussing what our respective next career moves might be, specifically what kind of restaurant we were interested in opening. I mentioned my then-nascent ideas about the restaurant on Nantucket, and my concern that the location on Main Street would bring with it certain expectations. I started rattling off the endless ways in which I could try to tailor the restaurant to appeal to the broadest number of people—pancake bar, juice bar, tartare bar, beach boxes—when she said, "You know, Kath, that's the difference between you and me: you want to be everything to everybody, and I don't feel I have to be." That I am guilty of trying to please everyone wasn't news to me, but for some reason, hearing myself described this way made me stop and think. I had always consciously tried to create the broadest appeal possible at my restaurants, but maybe now that I had established myself there was room for the Everything Girl to show some restraint. So for the first time, I altered the size of my menu. For example, since I was offering a pancake bar, the rest of my breakfast menu could be a lot smaller. I may start applying this lesson in restraint to my other concepts. You're never too old or experienced to learn something new.

After we open MET on Main, what then? Back when I was seeking out investors for Natick, my father said to me, "You have to grow the company to at least $40 million in order to sell it." Consequently, I struck a nontraditional deal with my investors, a plan to build the business to $40 million or $50 million dollars in revenue and then sell. Their return would come in the event of a sale. We would use the proceeds to build more restaurants and, of course, take loans if necessary. We have done that. We hope to grow the bar and grill/burger bar concept nationally and internationally. I think the concept and the numbers warrant that kind of growth. We are entertaining several opportunities as I write.

In the far-off future, I'd like to carry on my father's legacy, selling the company and then acting as an angel investor and advisor to the new Todd Englishes of the world. I've got a ways to go. In seven years I've doubled the value of my company, but I won't open another restaurant unless it makes sense, so I've probably got another five to ten years before hitting the benchmark he set (I'm about halfway there, Dad). And if we don't get there, I won't be disappointed. We'll run the restaurants we have and just become better and better at it.

It will be interesting to see how we navigate the town's and everyone else's expectations once we open on Main Street. Nantucket has a sense of community that Carl and I have been missing. As we watch the island wake up from its sleepy hibernation, we are meeting all sorts of fascinating characters, local and summer people alike. It has been a remarkably positive experience so far. And it feels good to be part of something, together.

At fifty-five, you see the world differently than you did at forty. You let things roll in a way you never could before; you have the ability to recognize what you have and appreciate it;

you gain a bird's-eye perspective about what matters and what doesn't in the whole damn grand scheme of things. The true gift of Nantucket has been taking this magical journey with Carl. Ten years ago we bought a piece of land in Monomoy with dreams of building our family summer home there. We have gotten a little waylaid, as we have been busy building our restaurant dream instead of our dream house. But this restaurant venture has taken us to the island in the most unexpected way. When we were negotiating the deal, it never occurred to us that we would take such pleasure leaving behind our big home in Brookline to live in a modest one-bedroom apartment overlooking the terrace of MET on Main.

Our happiness with our life on Nantucket speaks volumes about what is important in life. Human connection. Intimacy. Being supported. Supporting someone else. When you have those things, you have everything. The girl who grew up in the big house on the hill knew that all the stuff money can buy can never bring you happiness, but it's nice to be reminded in such a powerful way. Money buys comfort, peace of mind, and the freedom to move, but nothing rivals the internal peace I feel when taking a morning walk down Main Street in the fog for a cup of coffee with the person you love, or sharing that first bite of a delicious hand-rolled waffle cone from The Juice Bar, or taking an afternoon drive out to the beach at Great Point, or (hopefully) listening to the sounds of a full, buzzy patio at MET on Main wafting through my windows on summer nights.

I started this business to gain my independence and to secure my family's future, but I also had a lot to prove to my dad, to my mom, and to myself. Being able to contribute to something bigger than myself has been an awesome experience. Creating something that people are willing to pay for, to spend their hard-earned money on, is a mind-blowing endorsement. MET Club, MET Bar & Grill, MET Back Bay, and MET on Main—all are venues where people can come together to share food and enjoy being with friends and family, all are venues designed to provide to others what I believe is most important in life.

Though it has taken almost eight years for me to get this far in the restaurant business, I started preparing for the life I was to lead many years ago, when I was at my nana's apron strings. It turns out that the best education you can get is from living fully and well, learning from your mistakes, listening to others, and conquering your fears. I started out wanting to grow a big business, and I'm well on my way, but ultimately I'm the one who has grown the most in the eight years since I first embarked on my restaurant dreams—in confidence, in fearlessness, in problem-solving capabilities, in my ability to trust my intuition, and in my capacity to have fun in the midst of all the hard work. There is deep satisfaction in looking around and realizing that you've accomplished your vision, let alone built a viable business. It has not been an easy ride, but it has been one hell of a fun journey. I am not sure what will happen next, but I look forward to the challenges. What I do know is that I have come close to finding my master recipe for happiness.